Bicycles

obsessions

David Perry

David Perry joined his first cycling team at the age of 4, and has been competing and collecting bikes ever since. He is the author of *Bike Cult: The Ultimate Guide to Human Powered Vehicles*, and owner of Bike Works NYC.

Bicycles

obsessions

David Perry

hardie grant books

Contents

Why be obsessed
with bicycles?

When a person takes an interest in bikes and cycling it can easily become a career, a hobby or a lifestyle thing – a way of living and a reason for being. When cyclists speak of 'living the life', it's usually having the opportunity to just ride, eat and sleep. Whatever a cyclist's proclivities, bicycles are a way to indulge in one's passion and get the most out of living. With a bike, what you put in is what you get out.

Bicycles are bodily appendages that enhance daily movement and travel, and owners can often become physically and spiritually attached to them. Simply owning a second-hand beater bike, or acquiring a new one, can bring a warm, fuzzy feeling. Some cyclists give their bikes pet names and dress them up with stickers, ribbons or floral accoutrements. Whether it's through colourful handlebar tape or a fresh paint job, customizing your bicycle provides more personal intimacy with your machine.

Some of the best attributes of cycling are the freedom, independence and self-sufficiency that come from riding a pedal-powered vehicle. People love getting around by their own means. Some obsess about saving money and saving the planet. Others love to explore their favourite places – scenic roads, waterfront paths or mountain trails, both local and far away.

Another unique aspect of cycling is the sensation of flying. Whether one is speeding downhill on tarmac roads or catching air off a dirt jump, the feeling of flight plays a big part in the culture of bikes. Each generation of new cyclists seems intent on surpassing the limits of gravity for the next adrenaline rush. Once a kid gets the hang of bike riding, the first show of mastery is often to go 'no hands' on the handlebar.

The benefits of cycling are well established and it can be perfect for a maintaining a healthy lifestyle. Cycling offers a full range of activity for all fitness levels – from using the least to the most energy, or choosing the easiest or most difficult route – and every rider finds a balancing point along the way. For many, just chilling out while riding home after a stressful day is good enough medicine.

Many enthusiastic cyclists have a room or garage dedicated to their bikes. This is where the ready-to-ride and project bikes mingle with frames, parts, wheels, tyres, tubes and tools. Alongside the bikes there may be rollers, home trainers or an online fitness machine for stationary spinning. Then there are the extra cabinet drawers for cycling apparel, shoes and helmets, plus heaps of water bottles and nutritional supplements.

For people who love machines and technology, the bicycle inspires a can-do, hands-on ingenuity and inventiveness that keeps new designs and products coming. Each generation has its curious bike fads and confounding technical leaps. Niche trends explode in popularity, such as the mountain bikes of the early 1980s and the fixed-gear bikes of the early 2000s. Now we're in a time of wide-tyre, electronic-geared, hydraulic disc brake 'groads' – or gravel-road bikes. Who knows what's next?

1

Fundamentals

A sum of its parts

The bicycle is one of the best inventions of the modern age. As a wheeled extension of our bodies, it is one of the most efficient means of transport and offers the most enjoyable of sports. The combination of body, machine, mind and journey gives bikes and cycling a synergy that's reflective of the search for freedom and perfection in the human spirit.

Bicycles reflect the human form; they come in all varieties of form, shape, size, quality and hierarchy. Each bike has a purpose in life, designed by the maker for the needs of a cyclist. While transportation is the main purpose of a bike, to a large extent the sport of cycling, with its various branches and governing bodies, has influenced the styles and innovations we see in bikes today.

A complete bicycle is the sum of its parts and you want the best-quality materials and manufacture possible. Bicycles are assembled from dozens of components and thousands of individual parts that comprise the whole machine. The frameset – a frame and fork – is the chassis for the components and accessories, including the cyclist's three contact points (the handlebar, saddle and pedals), the wheels, drivetrain, brakes, controls, mudguards, kickstands, racks, lights, bags, bottle holders and repair kits that complete a fully equipped bicycle.

▶ Harry Lawson's 1879 bicyclette, a forebear of modern bicycle engineering.

Components of a bicycle

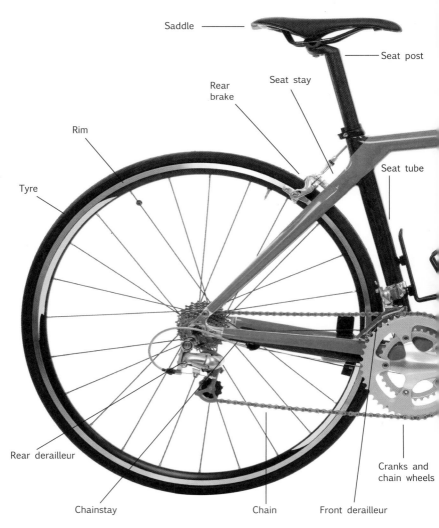

Saddle

Seat post

Seat stay

Rear brake

Rim

Seat tube

Tyre

Rear derailleur

Cranks and chain wheels

Chainstay

Chain

Front derailleur

Stem

Handlebar

Gear lever

Head tube

Top tube

Brake lever

Down tube

Front brake

Fork

Pedal

Spokes

Hub

15

Materials

Hardened steels are used for axles, bearings, nuts and bolts, while various steel alloys are used for frame tubing, lugs and fittings. These include high-tensile steel, chrome molybdenum and stainless steel.

Aluminium is widely used in frames, forks and most lightweight components. CNC machining, a manufacturing process that involves the use of computers to control machine tools, is used for finishing details and speciality components.

Titanium is a relatively rare non-ferrous metal that combines high strength, light weight, resilience and anti-corrosion. It's been used for derailleurs, stems and axles. For frame building, pure titanium is alloyed with aluminium and vanadium and then rolled into tubes, and joined by TIG welding.

▼ A quick-release bicycle wheel axle.

Carbon fibre is a plastic-like composite of graphite, carbon or boron fibres made in sheets impregnated with blends of epoxy resin that is layered, moulded, pressed, cured and hardened into any desired shape.

Framesets

Bicycle framesets are made of various materials, each with its special joining methods. The highest-quality bikes are made from various alloys of steel, aluminium, titanium, carbon fibre composite and even wood, such as bamboo. Choosing the best frame material depends as much on one's budget as one's desired qualities – whether these be lightness, strength or ride quality.

Steel is the most common material for a frame and has been developed to ever-higher standards of alloy and treatment. Steel is easier to repair than the other frame materials, and is offered in many qualities of tube shape, each rolled to fit a particular type of bike. The firms Reynolds and Columbus originally made classic lugged frame tubesets, then new kinds of tube were developed for popular TIG-welded joints from Tange and Tru Temper tubing.

▼ A 2011 Specialized 'Allez' road racing bicycle frame.

Aluminium frames are typically TIG welded and heat treated, often with the weld bead smoothed out to make a seamless joint. Early carbon composite frames were assembled in a jig with traditional

round tubes bonded into aluminium or steel lugs. Monocoque (meaning 'single shell' in French) frames are made in a mould as a single sculpture, requiring a different mould for each frame size.

When choosing frame size, the basic starting point is standover height – the distance from the ground to the top tube – followed by the height of the seat tube (the frame tube that contains the seat post of the bike and connects to the saddle, see pages 14–15). But equally important, if not more so, is the length of the top tube. This is the frame tube that runs horizontally from the top of the head tube to the seat cluster. This measurement determines the reach from saddle to bars, and the setback from pedals to saddle.

Cycling positions

Finding a proper or ideal cycling position requires careful consideration of the cyclist's physicality, flexibility, pedalling style, typical clothing, shoes and height. There are bikes designed for seemingly every body position possible, from standing upright to lying prone, facing backwards. Somewhere in between are the four general cycling positions and types of bike: upright roadster, middle-bend trekker, bent-over racing and laid-back recumbent.

The upright roadster posture provides a relaxed ride with easy mounting and dismounting. A middle-bend trekking position supports a more active ride

that allows the cyclist to stand on the pedals and pull on the handlebar. The bent-over racing style offers a more aerodynamic and powerful cycling position. It allows the cyclist to alternate between standing for climbing, sitting back for cobblestones and tucking for downhill descents.

In a laid-back recumbent cyclists ride with an upright back and legs forward, while a low-rider allows the cyclist to be in an extremely supine position. Then you launch into the prone and backward-facing machines with aerodynamic fairings, which are the world's fastest bicycles.

Handlebars

The handlebar and stem are clamped to the steering tube of the front fork and wheel. Most bars are made of tubular chrome steel, aluminium alloys or carbon composite, though a rare option is laminated wood. There are countless shapes of handlebar designed for form, function and fashion. Most are chosen for a particular riding style or preferred hand positions. The width of your shoulders and the obstacles you come across are also determining factors.

Drop bars on road bikes curve from the top forwards and down, where hands rest beside the stem. The hand position in drops is for sprinting, while hands on brake lever hoods are best for climbing. Classic road bars may have deep or shallow drops; Randonneur touring bars have tops that curve upwards from the stem; ergonomic bars have slight bends, added for comfort; track- or pista-style drops used for sprinting have a fully curving bend; and flat-top drop bars provide a forearm rest for a quasi-time trial position.

More upright handlebars include moustache bars, which are like flattened drop bars that curve forwards; porteur bars, which are relatively flat and sweep back towards the rider; and common roadster touring bars, which sweep back and rise with an outward splay like wings.

Mountain bikes have riser bars, with a variety of rise, sweep and diameter sizes. BMX bikes use higher riser bars, often with a crossbar, which is the same as some downhill mountain bikes. (They have the most fortified bars.) The defining features of a handlebar are its bends, whether they are hard angles or natural curves. One of the coolest styles is the single-arm bar, with brake and gear levers that swivel every which way. This is found on the Windcheetah recumbent tricycle designed by Mike Burrows.

Saddles

A fundamental contact point of the body to the bike, the seat, or saddle, is purposely designed for sitting on while pedalling. Saddle shapes are typically based on a cyclist's riding style and torso angle. Various saddles have been invented to conform to the shape of the sit bones of the pelvis. A cyclist can choose his or her desired amount of hardness or cushion by picking different kinds of foams or gels on the top of the saddle, and elastomers and springs underneath.

Leather saddles act as hammocks that suspend a rider. They are assembled by stretching a piece of shaped hide between the nose at the front and the cantle at the rear and are usually attached with rivets. Most offer adjustable tension by moving the nose relative to the rails. To provide even more suspension, many leather saddles have double and triple sets of springs as part of their undercarriage.

Anatomic saddles have a depression or cut-out in the middle to prevent pressure on the perineum. Female-specific saddles are usually short and wide, although plenty of women use men's or unisex saddles. Most saddles are designed to be set up at a level position, the top horizontal to the ground. Men seem to prefer their leather saddles angled nose up, while women are inclined to have the nose slightly lower.

Pedals

Good-quality bicycle pedals are important, as the full weight of a cyclist is often applied to one pedal when starting, dismounting or scooting a bike. Pedals with precision bearings and minimal platform height are ideal. Everything is available, from platform pedals with rubber pads for riding barefoot or with soft-sole shoes to bear-claw rat traps for extra shoe grip.

Traditional road quill pedals have small notches, to keep cycling shoes centred, and toe clips and straps, both to keep the shoe from slipping on the pedal's downstroke and to aid with a certain amount of pulling on the upstroke. Toe clips with various wire shapes and zoomorphic designs have been around since the nineteenth century. Half clips have no straps for easy entry and exit of the foot.

Clipless pedals are popular for serious cycling – being a shoe, cleat and pedal system that's comfortable, efficient and relatively safe. They come in two basic formats: one with two-bolt cleats for casual and mountain bike shoes, and the other with three-bolt cleats for road and track riding. The pedals and cleats typically offer adjustable release tension and either a fixed position or a certain degree of flex, called float, to allow for pronation in the pedal stroke.

▲ A triathlete can save time by clipping cycling shoes to the pedals.

Wheels

Modern bicycle wheels are marvels of engineering, having a load-to-weight ratio of around 400:1. Wheels come in many sizes and speciality shapes, depending on the kind of bike and riding. Despite the common use of automated wheel-building machines and the development of wild new designs and materials, there remains a practical mystique of a bicycle wheel made by hand using traditional methods.

A typical wheel is comprised of a central hub laced with spokes that attach to a hoop-like rim with spoke nipples. The hub fits to the bike frame and the rim fits to a tyre. Hubs have axles of various size, for front and rear wheels, with ball bearings in loose, retainer or sealed cartridges, the best being grade 25 steel or lightweight ceramic, that spin faster with less effort. Hub shells have small or large flanges to hold the spokes, with any number of spoke holes from 16 to 72, while 32- and 36-spoke holes are standard.

▶ Custom-made wheels sit on racks at the Detroit Bikes manufacturing facility in Michigan, USA.

Spokes hold the wheel laced together between the hub and rim. Most high-quality bikes have stainless-steel spokes, with J-hook or straight pull heads and straight gauge, double-butted or bladed shapes. Other spoke materials, like titanium, carbon fibre and aluminium are on the cutting edge of lightweight technology. Nipples are made in basic chromed brass or lighter aluminium alloy, the best with a thread-locking component to prevent loosening.

A rim is distinguished by its cross-section – whether box-section, v-section or deep-section; by its spoke holes – with single or full eyelets or washers; and by basic factors like weight, material and braking surface. Disc wheels have fully covered sides for optimal aerodynamics in competition on road, track and triathlon bikes. Front and rear disc wheels are used for indoor track events; usually only rear disc wheels are used outdoors, since sidewinds can topple a cyclist.

Tyres

Bicycle tyres are like shoes in that they are made for all kinds of surfaces, from wood floors to greasy tarmac and gravel. Tyres are categorized by the way in which they attach to the rim, as clinchers or tubulars; the way they hold air – with inner tubes, tubeless sealant, or semi-solid airless; and also by the type of tread, be it slick, grooved or knobby. The buoyancy of air-filled pneumatic tyres offers suspension, the sidewall casing allows balance and turning, and the longitudinal tread provides traction and braking. Given how much good tyres can do, it's amazing how small the contact patch on a bicycle tyre is.

▶ Hutchinson's Urban Tour Serenity tyre is 100% puncture proof.

Clincher tyres are the most common because they're easy to repair or replace. The tyre casing is separate from the tube, and is mounted to the rim as the tyre's bead is seated in the bead seat of the rim. A rim strip covers the spoke nipples or spoke holes in the rim and must not be pushed aside or caught in the bead seat.

Tubular tyres are the ultimate tyres for performance and retro rides. Handmade tubulars can be slender or wide, slick or knobby. Tubulars have the casing sewn together with the tube inside and a base layer that is glued to the rim with rim cement or highly adhesive rim tape. Tubulars offer unsurpassed suppleness and minimal rolling resistance in high- or low-pressure applications for road, track and cyclo-cross racing, as well as gymnasium cycle sports.

Tubeless tyres are available with tubeless specific rims for mountain, cyclo-cross and road bikes. They have no tubes, only a special bead that, when inflated, snap-fits to a rim with a smooth gutter and a fortified valve fitting. They are not puncture proof, but tubeless sealant can be injected into the tyre to help close small leaks. Another problem is burping: when the tyre bead 'burps' and air pressure drops.

The pneumatic tyre allows an air-cushioned ride at the expense of an occasional puncture. Few people enjoy getting a flat tyre, unless it gives an excuse to stop on a hard ride! To fix it on your own requires a pump, tyre levers and either a patch kit, a spare tube or a spare tyre. Non-pneumatic or semi-pneumatic tyres are puncture proof at the expense of buoyancy and ride quality. The 100% puncture-proof, Hutchinson Urban Tour Serenity tyres, have an aerospace polymer insert, no valve and no need ever to inflate, and rides like it's 60 psi.

Tyre and rim sizes

Countless tyre and rim sizes have been made for bicycles. Manufacturers in different countries, like the UK, France, the Netherlands, Germany, Scandinavia and Italy, produced their own tyre and rim sizes before standards were set by the European Tyre and Rim Technical Organization (ETRTO) in the 1960s and adopted by the International Standards Organization (ISO) in the late 1970s. It was common to find two or more tyres with the same nominal size that fit completely different rim sizes.

The diameter of the tyre must match that of the rim, but the width of the tyre can be any size within the range suitable for the width of the rim, typically 1.5 to 2 times the rim width. Most tyres and rims are referred to by their nominal size based on outside diameter and tyre width. This is not the true measure, just a close designation. These numbers are either fractional or decimal inches or metric sizes.

French metric tyres are measured by diameter in millimetres, and by width in letters (A, for example, is narrow at 20 mm, while D is wide at 50 mm). An exception came with narrow 700-size clincher tyres designated as C.

British tyres and rims had a letter and number system to designate size, such as E.3, EA1, F8 and K.2, and America's Schwinn bikes used an S followed by a number, like S-6. The most exact tyre measures are the bead seat circumference, the length in millimetres around the tyre bead or bead seat diameter (BSD), where the tyre bead seats into the rim.

The standard way of measuring a rim is diameter and width, the diameter being the BSD, and the width being the inner rim width – the distance between the two hook flanges of the rim.

Despite the international standards, there are still occasional problems fitting a tyre properly to a rim, especially when mixing new production tyres with vintage rims that may not have the appropriate hook-bead type fitting. Narrow 700C tyres with thick casing and tread can be very difficult to mount on certain rims, particularly getting that last section of bead over the rim's edge without pinching the inner tube. Other tyres may sit a bit too large on a rim. When fully inflated, the inner tube can erupt from under the tyre bead and bulge out of the rim. The remedy is using thicker layers of rim tape to close the gap.

Below are typical bike types and the sizes of their tyres:

BIKE TYPE	NOMINAL SIZE	ISO / ETRTO SIZE	BEAD CIRCUMFERENCE
Tall roadster	28 x 1-1/2"	47–635	1994
Vintage sport	27 x 1-1/4"	35–630	1978
XL MTB	29 x 2.3"	60–622	1955
Road	700 x 23	23–622	1955
Roadster	26 x 1-3/8"	37–590	1854
Large MTB	27.5 x 2.2"	52–584	1835
Touring	26 x 1-1/2" 650B	40–584	1835
Small road	26 x 1" 650c	23–571	1794
Standard MTB	26 x 2.125"	54–559	1755
Small roadster	24 x 1-3/8"	40–540	1695
Small MTB	24 x 1.75"	47–507	1592
Folding	20 x 1-3/8"	37–451	1416
BMX	20 x 1.95"	50–406	1274

Drivetrains

Bicycle gears have evolved tremendously in the 150 years since the first velocipedes. Chain drives had been developed by 1890, then came coaster brakes, freewheels and internal hub gears at the start of twentieth century. It took another generation or two for derailleur systems to come into common use.

A bicycle's drivetrain transfers pedal power to multiply the rotations of the drive wheel. It consists of a crankset, including the bottom bracket bearings, crank arms and chain wheels, a chain or belt, and the sprockets on a drive wheel.

▶ Racing bike rear derailleur sprocket gears.

Internal hub gears have a system of epicyclic gears inside the drive-wheel hub that provides multiple speeds, or gear ratios, with the flick of a lever. On a typical three-speed hub there's low gear, direct drive and high gear. Hub gears are a tidy system, but they are heavier than derailleurs in terms of grams per gear.

Derailleur gear systems push the chain off one sprocket and onto another. As the chain adjusts to different sprocket sizes it needs to keep its proper tension. The rear derailleur keeps the chain tensioned with spring-loaded jockey wheel cages. It shifts across the sprockets on the drive-wheel hub, in a parallelogram that's limited by high- and low-adjustment screws.

In the past hundred years, the number of rear cogs has increased from four to eleven. With two or

three front sprockets, there are plenty of wide ratios available for any terrain. Narrow chains and slim-tooth cassettes took over from freewheels in the days of eight speeds as the standard for rear hubs. Gear-changing systems have often been proprietary, so they are not always interchangeable with similar products of other brands. For good or bad, all the big makers produce proprietary systems.

Foot-operated brakes

The simplest kind of brake is that operated by the foot in a backward-pedalling motion. The fixed-gear brake works by resisting the forward motion of pedal cranks, with gradually increasing pressure or with a sudden forceful effort to lock up the rear wheel, known as a skid stop.

The coaster brake is an easier way to skid stop than a fixed gear. It's a mechanism in the hub made of various plates, shoes or cones that clutch the hub shell when reverse motion of pedal cranks is applied, causing the wheel to slow or stop. Its big disadvantage is that when the rider is stopped, there's no backpedalling, so it's difficult to move the pedals to a position that's easy to start again from.

In the 1930s, hubs for coaster-brake cruiser bikes had multiple flanges to dissipate heat. While foot-operated brakes are dependent on a chain properly connected and tensioned to the drive wheel, they are relatively impervious to weather and easy to use.

Hand-operated brakes

Caliper-operated rim brakes are a popular brake system for most lightweight bicycles. Brake calipers come in various configurations, including stirrup, side-pull, centre pull, dual pivot, cantilever, direct or linear pull, U-mount and roller cam. Calipers are spring-loaded arms mounted to the bicycle's frame and fork, fitted with brake shoes that are positioned to make contact with the front or rear wheel rim. They are activated by the brake lever, usually mounted on the handlebar, through a system of either rods and levers, cables and housing, or hydraulic fluid lines.

Cantilever brakes are a type of brake designed for more tyre clearance and stopping power. There are two types: standard centre-pull cantilever and direct or linear pull, often called V-brakes (appropriating Shimano's brand name). Both have left- and right-pivoting spring-loaded arms mounted to studs on fork blades and seat stays. The centre-pull variety has arms that protrude outwards and a straddle cable and hanger. The cable from the brake lever pulls the straddle cable up as the arms and pads pull inwards towards the rim. The tricky part is keeping it centred by adjusting the straddle and spring tension. Direct or linear pull brakes have tall arms that pull together from one side, with the cable housing stop on one arm and cable clamp on the other.

Drum brakes have been used for many years on classic, practical and load-carrying bikes. Inside

▶ A disc
brake on the
back wheel
of a bicycle.

the hub is a drum encircled by a belt-like pad that provides friction. They are relatively waterproof, very reliable and consistent, but somewhat heavier than rim brakes. Drum brakes can be mounted to front or rear wheels, but because of the increased force and leverage, the front forks must be fortified.

Disc brakes have become more and more popular because of their better performance, especially in extreme conditions. A disc brake has a frame- or fork-mounted caliper with pads that squeeze against a rotor fixed to the hub shell. Today there are basic cable-operated mechanical calipers and special multi-piston hydraulic calipers, with various forms of floating calipers and pads and all kinds of rotor sizes (from 140 mm to 220 mm), materials (stainless steel, titanium, aluminium) and cut-out shapes. They require a disc-specific frame and fork with special mounts for the calipers; disc-specific hubs with special mounts for disc-shaped rotors; and disc-specific racks with wider legs for caliper-mount clearance.

After problems of ejecting front wheels on bikes with standard fork ends and quick-release skewers, special fork tips and through-axle hubs have developed. The pros and cons of disc brakes are widely discussed, as rotors have now appeared on the wheels of World Tour road racing bikes.

Types of bike

Each kind of bike has a frame and components
tailored for its use. The elegant upright roadsters
keep a rider's clothes clean with full chain cases,
mudguards and skirt guards. A typical city bike-
for-hire has similar features but in a one-size-fits-all
format. Touring bikes are sportier roadsters with
a special selection of components and accessories,
including wide-ratio gearing, load-carrying racks at
the front and rear, polychrome fenders and dynamo-
powered LED lighting. There are fully equipped

touring bikes for daily commuting, camping trips and exploratory adventures.

Tandem and triplet bikes allow couples and threesomes to ride together on two-wheeled machines. Cargo bikes are dedicated to hauling large loads for delivering or transporting people, pets, plants and shopping goods. The long wheelbase fortified frames are half-bike, half-carrier rack, with sophisticated gearing, brakes and steering linkages. Loads are usually placed in front of the cyclist on two-wheelers, while bikes with loads behind include long-rack Xtracycles, trailer bikes and traditional trailers with one or two wheels. Cargo trikes may have loads over the dual front steering wheels or the rear driving wheels.

◀ A tandem has seats and pedals for two riders – allowing couples to share the strain.

Road bikes

Road racing bikes rarely have mudguards, but they have the best component groups with better wheels, gears, brakes and controls, enabling maximum performance and speed. The same goes for track-racing bikes, where only the single gear is fixed and there are no brakes. The pinnacle of this breed are the nimble and sturdy NJS-approved track sprint bikes employed in Japan's Keirin pari-mutuel bicycle racing, in which spectators bet on races and there can be no equipment advantage among the cyclists.

Both road- and track-racing bikes also have special time-trial machines for individual and team timed events, with disc wheels, multi-platform handlebars and streamlined framesets. Once named 'funny bikes' because they require that the rider assume a Superman position, the epitome of this type are all the UCI world hour record bikes from Colnago and Pinarello, as well as all the world championship triathlon bikes.

A road bike not designed for racing can have flat-top or riser handlebar controls, disc brakes and bits of touring accessories. A hybrid bike is a practical upright type of all-purpose vehicle. A fixie is the street version of a track bike; a pure one has no brake, only direct drive to stop. It has riser bars or bullhorn handlebars, platform pedals and colourful rims, tyres and chains for sex appeal. A single-speed is any bike with a single-sprocket freewheel for transmission, to keep it simple and sturdy.

Recumbent bikes

Recumbent bikes offer cyclists a laid-back reclined riding position. They are categorized by length, position, steering and drivetrain. Long wheelbase (LWB) recumbents have the pedals behind the front wheel for a stable ride; short wheelbase (SWB) bents have the pedals in front of the front wheel for a nimble, quick-steering ride and compact long wheelbase (CLWB) models have the pedals over or near the front wheel for steady handling.

▼ Windcheetah recumbent tricycle designed by Mike Burrows.

There are chopper style semi-recumbents with lower pedals and higher seats, and lowracer recumbents with supine seats and higher pedals. There's over-seat steering (OSS), above-seat steering (ASS), under-seat steering (USS) and pivoting boom steering (PB), like the Flevo. Most are rear-wheel drive (RWD) but a growing share are front-wheel drive (FWD) bikes. One type has the cranks fixed to the frame with a twisting chain when steering, another has cranks fixed to the fork with turning pedals when steering.

Off-road bikes

Off-road riding brought features from motorcycles, such as suspension systems, hydraulic disc brakes and tubeless tyres. Cyclo-cross bikes are rigid-frame, 'off-road' road bikes, with a separate category of components, such as cantilever brakes with top-mount brake levers, compact cranksets and medium-wide tubular tyres with knobby tread patterns. A cross-country mountain bike usually has a rigid frame and suspension fork, known as a hard tail, for moderate trial riding and racing.

▼ BMX bikes typically have smaller wheels for racing and stunts.

Downhill mountain bikes are full-suspension machines intended for high-speed cycling on steep rocky trails. These bikes have dual crown forks with 7" to 10" of suspension travel, extra large disc brake rotors, and various chain guides and gearbox

transmissions to withstand the bumps and shocks of descending from steep drops. Freeride bikes offer a lighter, more nimble version of a pure downhill machine that can climb, jump and balance better.

Freestyle and dirt jumping bikes come in three wheel sizes (20", 24" and 26"), with single-speed micro gearing (25 x 9) and a rear rim brake only. Trial bikes are pure stunt riding bikes, typically with a wide range of gears. As a true example of specialization, some trials bikes are designed without a saddle.

BMX bikes are made for racing and stunt riding on smaller wheels (16" to 24") in the dirt or on vert, pump track, street or flatland. Starting in the early 1970s, like mountain bikes, BMX is now an Olympic sport with a historic tradition in which the old-school bikes and parts have become collectibles.

Fat bikes are a relatively new category designed for riding on sand and snow, with extra wide frames, hubs, rims, and tyres that range from 3.5" to 4.8" wide. These are not super-fast bikes; the thrill comes from surpassing the most sluggish terrains on Earth.

A completely different kind of off-road category are all the bikes made for field, courtyard, abandoned railways, and for indoor cycling. Polo bikes are made for the team ball sport, played on grass or hardcourt, that's been revived in recent years. The bikes have a short wheelbase, low single-speed gearing and DIY wheel covers for blocking and swatting the street hockey ball.

What's collectible?

Everyone has their favourite vintage bicycle based on the first kind that turned them onto bikes and cycling. Maybe you couldn't get the one you wanted as a child but have been able to attain it as an adult. Whatever the reason for wanting an older bike, they tend to roll through generations of cyclists, being loved by cyclists who are almost as old as they are.

This inter-generational admiration starts with the oldest members of the bike community, who may have cherished a four-speed Raleigh Record Road Ace of 1939, or a younger one fascinated by that period and wants to go on a Tweed ride. The baby boomer generation of the 1970s bike boom has made the classic lightweight vintage market active, partly due to parents

handing down their old bikes to their children, who learn to love them as well. There were the Sting-Rays, Krates and Choppers, then the American, British, French or Italian road bikes.

For a while, the trend was forty-somethings paying high prices for early BMX bikes and components. The latest trend is thirty-somethings who want classic upright roadsters – omafiets – with drum brakes, chain case, front basket and rear rack, or vintage French hammered-fender randonneur bikes made well before they were born.

▼ Below: Cinelli Supercorsa (1972).
▶ Right: Schwinn Sting-Ray Apple Krate (1970s); bottom right: Gios Torino Professional (1986).

2

Accessories
& Apparel

All the extras

The breadth of bicycle-related accessories and apparel is astounding, and all items are designed to fit the active nature of this vehicle. Other than the frame, wheels and components, everything else for bikes and cycling is an accessory or article of clothing. The finest bikes usually come fully equipped with fenders, bags, baskets, racks, lights, locks and bells. These may be fixed securely to the bike, sometimes as part of the bicycle's design, or they can be detachable and removed for occasional use.

Bags

The variety of carrying sacks for bikes and cyclists include backpacks, fanny packs and hydration packs; messenger bags, musette bags and saddlebags; handlebar bags, pannier bags and frame bags; trunk bags, tool bags and race kit bags; wheel bags and bike bags. These come in a full range of sizes for packing a repair kit, wallet, phone, camera, briefcase, computer, extra clothing, groceries, camping gear and more.

Wearable bags, such as backpacks and messenger bags, are only recommended when the bike has no carrying facility. Although it's best to carry heavy items on the bike itself, many cyclists prefer carrying their load on their body.

Simple handlebar and saddlebags strap to the front of the handlebar, while small saddlebags strap to the seat rails and seat post. Some of the better seats have two strap slots in the rear. With handlebar and saddlebags, the larger they are, the more they need a special decaleur fitting or rack for support. Most handlebar bags have a waterproof cover with a clear plastic sleeve for map reading.

Pannier bags are designed to clip onto a front or rear rack and offer the largest carrying capacity. They usually come in pairs, one bag for each side of the bike, but many people commute with only one. Deluxe panniers for camping trips have several side pockets and weatherproof covers. On a rear rack with two full side panniers, a tent and sleeping bag can fit between. To keep a bike that's loaded with dual front and rear panniers stable, it's always recommended to place the heaviest items as low as possible.

Baskets

▲ Baskets, once reserved for the more sedate cyclist, are now perfectly stylish.

Bike baskets are made of wire, wicker, plastic and wood. They're made to fit in front, attached to the handlebar and/or fork, or as part of a rear rack on top or at the sides. Rear-fitting side-rack baskets provide ample space in the two lower compartments and a wide platform on top. Some side-rack baskets fold in when not in use, for easier portability. A large finely woven wicker basket bespeaks of the richness of the goods being carried. Picnic-style baskets with handles and dual lids have quick-release fittings on rear racks. There are even baskets with padded liners designed for carrying pets.

Bells, horns & whistles

The musical sound of a bicycle bell is one of the bike's iconic features, even if it often goes unnoticed in a loud city. In most places, a noise-making warning device is required equipment on a bicycle for the safety of cyclists, motorists and pedestrians alike. Bells and horns are the most popular, while whistles are banned for cyclists in some places because they fit in the mouth and aren't as safe as other options.

Rotating bells make a short 'ding-a-ling' series of notes with a push of the lever. Some have rotating covers, while others rotate inside the bell. Single-stroke bells allow a more subtle ring and require multiple strikes to really get attention. Ding-dong bells are large and produce a two-note ring. Brass bells make the sweetest tones, and the nicer ones come plated in chrome or copper.

Air horns make sound by squeezing a bulb by hand or by releasing compressed air. The bulb type comes in trumpet and bugle shapes, but compressed air horns reach much higher decibels and attract more attention.

Carrier racks

Bicycle-mounted carrier racks can hold bags, baskets, child seats, boxes and even surf boards. Some racks are specially designed by the bike maker, using similar colouring and complementary shapes to the bike. Most racks are after-market add-ons and some are specifically designed for a certain wheel size and type of bag to be loaded. Light mounts and bungee cord hooks are also add-ons.

Motor-vehicle-mounted bicycle racks allow up to four bikes to be placed on the rear or top of a vehicle. Rear racks are designed to fit as many car shapes as possible. Roof racks are the professional way to go, as seen on road racing team cars, but can become a problem if the driver forgets how tall the bikes are when entering a garage, tunnel or underpass.

Child carriers

Child carriers come in various designs for children of different sizes and/or ages. Transporting one's most precious cargo in the safest possible way requires a high-back, slightly reclined seat, front brace, seat belts and foot holders. Some seats mount in front of the cyclist on the top tube and handlebar, while other seats mount to a rear rack behind the cyclist. Other kinds of child-carrying accessories include extra long cargo bikes, such as the Xtracycle with a long rear and top board for two kids, and the Bakfiets front carrier with bench seats and wood panels.

Computers

Before there were bicycle computers, there were cyclometers and speedometers. These measured distance and speed with gears and cables connected to display counters or dials – usually fitted to the front wheel – and counted rotations and frequency. With the electronic age came the first bicycle computers, powered by batteries, with a head unit mounted to the handlebar and a wire running to a magnetic sensor in the wheel. These featured mode and function buttons and LCD displays showing speeds (current, average and maximum), distance (trip and total) and time (clock, stopwatch, trip and total).

Eventually more advanced features were added, like cadence (pedal speed) – which requires another wire for the crank arm sensor – altimeters (elevation change), thermometers (temperature), pacing (plus or minus the average), heart monitors (complete with chest strap) and wireless capability. The Shimano Flight Deck and Campagnolo ErgoBrain systems featured virtual cadence, gear combinations and audible pacing functions. These days, the features of cycle computers are merging with smartphone apps and dedicated GPS navigation devices to bring more mapping, travel info and security capability to bike handlebars. One such item is a bicycle-tracking chip that can be hidden on a bike, which transmits signals to alert the owner of the bike's location if it's stolen.

Setting up a computer means configuring time, distance units (miles or kilometres) and wheel circumference. For more accuracy than the standard tyre size in the manual, it's best to set the computer based on riding an accurately measured distance.

Mudguards

Mudguards (also known as fenders) are available in partial or full coverage shapes and are made of chromoplastic, aluminium alloy, stainless steel or laminated wood. A mudflap of rubber, leather or plastic may be placed on the end as a finishing touch. Clip-on mudguards can be used without the necessary clearance or fittings for proper ones. They don't offer as much protection as full-coverage mudguards, but they do keep the 'rooster tails' of wheel spray from drenching one's behind on a rainy-day ride.

Traditional and high-end metal mudguards can come in copper, gold or pewter colours and have surfaces that are grooved, fluted, hammered for a pebbly look, chrome plated or polished. Some are painted the same colour scheme as the bike. The finest handmade mudguards have moulded fittings for head and tail lights with dedicated electrical lines running hidden from end to end. Mudflaps (also called fender skirts or side panels) help reduce wheel spray and keep long dresses or coats from catching in the spokes. In countries where mudflaps are more common, they are made in a variety of colourful materials. On public bikes for hire, full mudflaps often become a mini billboard for promotion and advertising.

There is a slight possibility that front mudguards, when clogged with debris, can suddenly halt a bike and send the rider and bike cartwheeling forwards. To prevent this, some mudguards have a quick-release safety device in the fittings.

Locks

Bike theft is an under-reported crime, but when a person's bicycle is stolen, it feels like a good friend is gone, never to be seen again. Since the majority of bike theft occurs when a bike is parked in a public place, it's best to have a foolproof locking system.

The basic idea is to protect the most valuable parts of the bike first. For example, if you have to choose between locking the front wheel or the rear wheel, it's best to lock the rear because it costs more to replace. Bicycle locks come as flexible braided-wire cable locks, case-hardened steel-link chain locks, large-shackle D- or U-shaped locks and steel-plated foldable locks. Padlocks are combined with cables and chains in various sizes and levels of security. Wheel locks are keyed axle bolts and skewers that help reduce the burden of carrying extra locks. With these systems, the same key can be used on locks for the seat post binder, threadless stem bolt and caliper brake bosses. Seat locks usually have a thin cable or chain that loops through the frame. Among the DIY techniques are ball bearings glued into hex-shaped Allen bolts, hose-clamped and duct-taped quick-release skewers, and quick-stop bungee-cord locking.

Lights

Most countries require a white or yellow headlight and a red tail light for night riding. Countries like Germany and France require lights on certain new bikes sold. Most lights offer a flashing or blinking mode to save energy; however, these are not allowed in Germany and Holland, as they may be confused with emergency vehicles. For most cyclists, lights are used more for being seen by other road users than for seeing the path or road ahead. Lights for riding in darkness require more power and illumination, with both a wide-angle and distance-focused beam to illuminate the road surface.

In the old days, before electronic circuitry, dynamo hubs would shut off when the bicycle stopped and blow out light bulbs when it was going too fast. Now, with capacitors and diodes, these systems have stand lights that stay on when stopped and are protected from an overloading current. Most dynamo lighting systems have wiring that runs from generator to headlight to tail light. On the finest bikes, these wires are hidden in forks, frames and mudguards.

Handlebar grips & wraps

The handlebar should be covered with something that has good grip because it's where your hands control the bike's steering, gear changes and braking, and where bare or gloved hands pull, push, grasp and rest.

A basic handlebar tape wrap on drop bars should take seven to fourteen minutes from start to finish, depending on whether it's a track, road or triathlon bar. That includes wrapping two rolls of cloth or padded tape with finishing tape and bar plugs, but removing old tape and residue can add more than twice that time.

In the old days, road drop bars were wrapped starting on the tops near the stem, where the clamp bulge or sleeve is located, and finishing on the ends of the drops. The wrap was cut to the exact length necessary in order to fold into the handlebar so the bar plug would sit tight. These days, bars are wrapped in the opposite direction, starting at the drops and ending on the tops. The traditional method allowed clean, smooth tops, without the need for finishing tape. The reason for the change is that the overlapping, inward tape tended to roll up at the edge when bare or gloved hands rested on the curve. Now, the overlapping tape faces outwards on the top and forward-curve portion of the bar.

The starting position for a wrap is at the end of the drop, with the end of the bar tape on the underside pulled over and outwards, with half its width hanging over the end of the bar. The first half rotation runs perpendicular to the bar, then the following rotation begins the angled pull, with about half the bar tape's width covered with each rotation. The amount of overlap helps determine thickness. Straight sections are easy, but the bends require a kind of radial angled tape winding. Taping around brake levers is done by placing a small strip of bar tape to cover the bar clamp of the brake lever, making one or two diagonal crossovers, and leaving all edges under the brake hood. Finishing at the tops, the end is usually cut in the angle of the weave so the last rotation leaves an edge perpendicular to the bar. The end can be glued down with rim cement or, more commonly, wound tight with finishing tape, either the logo tape in the box, or a colourful accent of electrician's tape.

Wrapping bars is usually the finishing touch on a bike build. Speciality handlebar wraps include shellac-impregnated cloth tape finished with layers of twine. Tyre inner tubes can be cut in contour shapes to pad cloth tape. Harlequin wraps weave two or more tape colours into diamond shapes, as if plaiting pigtails. The VIP wrap involves stretching a clean piece of fabric or hide around the bar and brake levers, then stitching it together on the underside.

Unrolling tape and exposing the adhesive underside of the tape is handled with care so it doesn't stick to the top side and wind up into a ball. The tape must be kept perfectly clean until it's finished. Cork and plastic tapes should not be stretched too much because they can tear and break, although some tears can be hidden under thicker layers.

Pumps & pressure gauges

Since tyres need a certain amount of air pressure to ride efficiently, compressed air is needed to keep tyres at their recommended pressure. Tyre pressure is measured in pounds per square inch (psi) or bars, and can range from 30 psi on fat bike tyres to 200 psi on track bike tubular tyres.

There are portable and pocket-sized hand pumps for carrying on rides and larger floor pumps for use at home or at events. Alternatives to hand-operated pumps are foot pumps, motorized compressed air pumps and CO_2 inflators. Suspension pumps are another kind of hand pump, made for inflating suspension forks with a big dial pressure gauge and air-release valve.

Hand pumps have either an integral valve head fixed to the end of the cylinder or a separate flexible air hose for the valve head. The hose type makes it easier to fasten to the valve but is less efficient than an integral valve head.

The two most common valve stems are Schrader and Presta, and bicycle pumps usually have a valve head to fit both types. The rarer Woods (or Dunlop) valves fit the same as a Presta. Valve heads may have one hole that fits both sizes, with interchangeable inner parts, or two holes for both sizes. Presta valve adaptors allow a Schrader valve head to pump Presta valves. Many pump heads have a tightening lever that compresses rubber washers around the valve stem.

Frame-fit pumps are made to carry on the bike frame – either along the seat tube or under the top tube. The top of the handle and the end of the valve head are shaped to fit frame tubes, and a spring compresses the handle just enough for the pump to stay put. Custom bike makers may offer a matching pump in the same colours as the frame.

Floor or track pumps are sturdier and easier to use than hand pumps. They offer more air volume and attain higher pressure faster. They come in various cylinder heights with analogue dial or battery-operated digital pressure gauges placed near the top or bottom. A long hose connects the valve head to the cylinder. When something is wrong with the valve stem, the hose gets filled but not the tyre.

Carbon dioxide inflators are a quick and convenient way to refill tyres when one can't spare the time or energy to use a pump. Mostly favoured by mountain bikers in competition, CO_2 inflators have valve heads that connect to replaceable gas canisters, usually 16-gram cartridges.

▲ A bicycle pump, whether hand or foot, is a necessary accessory for all cyclists.

Repair kits & tools

Any self-respecting bike rider will know the workings of their bicycles and how to maintain them at home. For this, one needs the basic tools, including a tyre repair kit, lubricants, cleaners and various hex and box wrenches for making adjustments. Once you get further into bike repair and parts replacement, it might be time to splash out on a work bench, bike stand or table vice.

Component-specific tools include cable cutters and crimpers for fixing cables and housings, splined tools for removing cassettes and freewheels, and cutting, facing, chasing and pressing tools to install headsets and bottom brackets. Axle vices and cone wrenches are used for adjusting or overhauling hubs; spoke wrenches, dishing guides and truing stands are for truing and building wheels; and chain whips and lockring tools are for changing fixed-gear cogs. Torque wrenches that prevent under- or over-tightening of bolts are necessary for assembling high-quality, lightweight components.

A typical tyre repair kit has several inner tube patches, rubber cement, a sheet of sandpaper, two tyre levers and also some talcum powder to lubricate the tyre and tube. In bike shops, patching tubes has gone out of fashion, as has racers patching their tubular tyres. Nowadays, a brand new tube is installed even if the puncture is tiny.

Simple bicycle lubricants and cleaners include oils for the chain and moving parts, grease for bearings and dish soap and degreaser for cleaning parts. More advanced supplies include anti-seize compounds to prevent metal parts from bonding together and retaining compounds to lock threads and keep nuts and bolts from loosening. Assembly compounds are used for fitting carbon and titanium components, and, for cutting metal, there's cutting oil. Suspension shocks use various weights of oil and hydraulic brake lines need brake fluid or mineral oil.

Apparel

The technical nature of cycling calls for specific features in clothing, such as breathability, wicking ability, padding, aerodynamics, protection and a certain cut of fabric for the various cycling positions. Dressing in layers of clothing is recommended so that clothing can be added or removed as weather conditions change. When choosing the correct size of an item, it's best to check the size chart of individual clothing makers rather than assume sizes are standardized. Special cycling clothes include traditional team caps, chamois-lined shorts, padded gloves, protective helmets, pocket-back jerseys, cleated shoes, waterproof rain capes and crash-friendly, skin-saving shoulder, elbow, knee and shin armour. The golden rule of cycling clothing is there is no such thing as bad weather, just bad clothing.

Shorts

For riding all day, padded cycling shorts can usually make the most difference when it comes to comfort and efficiency. To avoid chafing and saddle sores, cycling shorts should have a chamois-like pad in the crotch, without the big seams that exist in regular shorts. Cycling shorts are meant to be worn without underwear. For some, this is part of their initiation into cycling. However, there are cycling briefs for those who prefer an extra layer.

Traditional cycling shorts were usually made of wool with a real chamois leather pad. Shorts were black so they wouldn't show dirt and grease. To keep shorts from falling, especially when soaked in rain water, suspenders were attached in lieu of elastic waistbands, which tend to constrict the diaphragm and prevent deep breathing. To prevent chafing, riders used to spread a whale-blubber cream on their crotch. Today, we have muscle-supporting shorts made of lycra-like materials, with fabric pads in the crotch and bib straps as suspenders. You can choose thick or thin chamois pads, medicated or vegan chamois butter and loose or leg-gripping cuffs.

▲ Padded shorts can prevent saddle soreness or calluses caused by friction and irritation.

Helmets

Helmets are made with a front and a rear and are meant to be worn level on the head, not tipped up or down. Dual side straps secure the helmet under the chin with a clasp. To help fit tightly, sweat pads and plastic straps allow tightening and loosening with a ratchet, depending if something is worn underneath, like a cap or balaclava.

Shoes

Cycling shoes benefit pedalling efficiency because, compared to regular, non-cycling shoes, the soles are stiffer, providing less flex and a solid platform for the feet. Pedals with toe clips and straps and clipless pedals with cleats that fit to the sole help keep the feet in place throughout the pedal stroke.

Shoes are designed for the various types of cycling. Road-racing shoes are made light and sleek for performance, off-road shoes have knobby soles and higher cuts, and street cycling shoes are stylishly casual, with flat soles that grip. Any type of shoe may have laces, Velcro straps or special bindings with ratchets and twist knobs, which allow the shoe to be tightened without stopping the bike. The cleats that engage with pedals have two- or three-bolt fittings. Road shoes come with a three-bolt fitting, while off-road and street shoes have a two-bolt fitting.

Cyclists often have a peculiar way of walking, which may be due to too much time spent in a bent-over position on a bike or because the cleats on the soles of their shoes make walking awkward, loud and occasionally slippery. Fitting cleat covers can help. But if you rated cycling shoes on a 'walkability' meter, road shoes would get the lowest score, off-road shoes might score somewhere in the middle and street shoes would score the highest.

▼ Shimano Women's WR31 SPD-SL Cycling Shoes 2013.

▼ Overleaf, a triathlete keeps his helmet close at hand during the ITU World Triathlon Series, 2014.

3

Fitting & Geometry

Understanding the right fit

A major factor affecting a person's enjoyment of cycling and his or her enthusiasm to continue is the fit between body and bicycle.

The golden rule of a bicycle fitting is to fit the bicycle to the body, not the other way around. The human body is highly adaptable, while the bicycle is a semi-adjustable mechanical device. It's not a good idea to choose a too-large or too-small bike frame and attempt to compensate with shorter or longer components. This can badly affect comfort, handling and biomechanics. When assembling a bike, it's best to have the frame, wheels and all the parts in dimensions that fit a person's size and preferred cycling position.

The geometry of the frame and fork determines the kind of bike, its purpose and handling, and the starting points at which those components and contact points are measured. The bike's 'geometry' is the measure of its chassis size, shape and dimensions, including wheelbase, seat and top tube length, head and seat tube angle, fork rake, bottom bracket height and more. Most mass-production bikes have a geometry chart that shows frame sizes with the relevant measures to achieve a proper fit.

Fitting

A bicycle fitting involves measuring a cyclist's body, his or her bike and the two together. For the body, the cyclist's height, weight, inseam, torso, arms, hands, legs, feet and head are measured. For the bike, the body's contact point components are measured, including saddle height, setback and angle, stem height, length and angle, handlebar width, reach and height, hand controls placement, crank length, foot placement and cleat position. Relatively small differences in length or angle in any of these parameters make a big difference in the comfort, handling and riding characteristics of a bike.

A proper fitting requires various tools, such as a stationary fit cycle for testing different riding positions, shoe cleat adjustment kits for precise installation of cleats and wedges, and an adjustable stem to find the best handlebar position. The most advanced sessions offer digital laser measuring tools, power meters, video feedback, biometric analysis and wind-tunnel testing. All of this data goes into a bike builder's CAD program that spits out a printout with stick-figure diagrams of the body and the bike.

▲ Goniometers are used in fittings to measure angles so that seat height allows the correct knee bend and so on.

The first rule in fitting is to make sure you can easily stand over the bike. Standover height is typically the measure from the floor to the top of the tube where the cyclist straddles the bike. It's recommended to have 6 cm or a few fingers of space between your crotch and the bike to make easy mounting and dismounting from the bike. Inseam is the measure

from the crotch to the floor, with the cyclist standing upright with bare feet about 5 cm apart. The exact point in the crotch is the two ischium bones.

The second rule is to make sure your reach from saddle to handlebar is a comfortable distance and position for controlling the bike. In most cases, a person's arm and torso lengths are about the same as his or her handlebar reach. Different handlebar shapes cater to a wide range of cycling positions available. Torso length is measured from the crotch to the manubrium (the top of the sternum), when the cyclist stands upright. Arm length is measured from the edge of the shoulder to the centre of a bar grasped by the hand in an upright fist, with elbows extended.

▲ At a fitting attention will be paid to the angles and distances between elbows, shoulders, hips, knees and ankles.

Fork rake & trail

To optimize the steering and handling of a bicycle, the head tube angle or steering axis is modified for a particular type of bike and kind of riding, as well as the fork rake and trail. Fork rake, or fork offset, is amount of offset of the wheel hub to the steering axis. When considered with head angle and wheel diameter, fork rake determines trail. Trail is the amount the tyre's contact patch falls behind the steering axis.

For various types of road bikes the fork offset ranges from 40 to 55 mm. With head angles ranging from 70 to 75 degrees, trail amounts range from 50 to 65 mm. The ideal combination of stability and agility is considered to be about 57 mm.

Roadsters and race bikes have head angles ranging from 55 to 75 degrees, and fork offsets range from 38 to 56 mm. Trail ranges from 50 to 65 mm, and the ideal combination of agility and stability is considered to be about 57 mm for standard road bikes.

It seems there are too many interrelated parameters and riding configurations to make suitable equations to adequately explain this phenomenon. It involves forth-order, non-linear, partial differential equations with variable coefficients that have yet to be completely solved. These variables include the location of the cyclist's mass, the geometry of the bike, the size, grip and firmness of the tyre's contact patch, the condition of the terrain and the speed of the cyclist.

Head angle

Rake

Trail

Handlebar reach is the distance from the top of the
saddle, usually at the longitudinal centre of the seat,
or from the point at which the seat tube intersects the
saddle to the centre of the handlebar where it clamps
to the stem. Equally important is the difference in
height of the saddle to the stem, the rise or drop
of the handlebars. On the frame, reach is mostly
influenced by top tube length, which has both an
actual and effective measure, depending on whether
the shape is square or sloping.

Leg lengths are divided at the knees, into two
measurements to check for differences in length. With
the cyclist sitting on a bench with his or her back to
a wall and thighs parallel with the floor, the thighs
are measured from the back of the buttocks to the
front of the kneecaps. The lower legs are measured
similarly from the tops of the knees to the bottoms of
the feet. These measurements help determine saddle
setback and pedal-cleat placement, a critical element
in pedalling mechanics and the distribution of weight
over the wheels.

Shoulder width is measured across the back of a
cyclist who is standing upright, with arms extended
forwards and hands in palms-down fists. This helps
choose handlebar width and determine the position
of grips. Hand size can be measured like glove
size, or with the hand clenching a bar of varying
diameters. This also helps determine how thick to
make the handlebar wrap. Head size is measured like
hat sizing (the circumference at the forehead) to help
fit helmets and any headwear underneath.

Geometry

Once a fitting is completed, the next step is to choose the bicycle's geometry. These are the numbers that describe the exact size and dimensions of the bicycle and the intended purpose and use for the machine. Different kinds of bike have refined geometries that suit the differing styles of cycling.

A custom, handmade bicycle often begins with a full-scale drawing and a specification sheet of the frameset. The creator of this drawing may be a designer whose prototype spec will be mass-produced in a factory, or it may be the actual builder and fabricator of a made-to-measure customized bicycle. The frame builder determines the geometry and handling characteristics, based on fork trail, fork rake, wheelbase length and bottom bracket height.

For a traditional lugged steel frame, the drawings and spec sheet indicate the make of tubing, the length, diameter, wall thickness, angles and bends of each tube, and blade and stay section, along with the types of fork crown, lugs, bottom bracket shell and dropouts. Clearances for tyres, brakes, mudguards and shoes are noted, as are invisible lines of geometry – such as the horizontal line between axles that indicates bottom bracket drop, or the extended head tube angle that intersects the floor and measures fork trail.

The spec sheet also indicates tube couplers, internal or braze-on cable guides, seat post binders, mounting eyelets, brake bosses, brake and chain stay bridges, pump pegs and the like. In the case of a moulded composite or monocoque frame, these design details are incorporated into the mould or attached in a finishing process. Each of these details is chosen to complement the form and function of the finished bicycle.

The front fork on a bike defines its ride. Choosing the best fork can be simple when all the parameters are known, including tyre size, steering tube height, fork blade length, crown race diameter, brake mount type, brake mount placement, wheel axle type, eyelets for racks and clearance for mudguards. Suspension forks need a special frame geometry that allows several centimetres of bounce and travel. The more extreme the terrain, the more the amount of suspension travel.

A second reference point for bike makers is the frame's bottom bracket, which sets a point of alignment for bottom bracket drop and front-end distance. Bottom brackets are usually raised higher for extra clearance, be it for track bikes in velodromes or mountain bikes on irregular terrains. They are lower for city roadsters, load-carrying touring bikes and cargo bikes. Other factors in the bicycle's stability and turning radius are the wheelbase and chainstay length.

A cyclist's body

The ideal bike position is as neutral as possible, with the cyclist's mass balanced over the wheels. In this position, there's no excess energy expenditure and the pedal stroke spins at optimal power and frequency – the perfect union of body and machine.

When sitting in the saddle, the pelvic region is the main point of support for the cyclist's body weight. On standard bikes, the contact points are usually the two ischium bones of the pelvis, which are cushioned by small fluid sacs called the ischial tuberosity. The ischium bones are typically about 7.5 centimetres apart for men and 10 centimetres apart for women, so saddles are designed accordingly. Recumbent bikes have seats with back rests, with contact points shared by the ischium, ilium and sacrum bones.

The position of the torso and shoulders, or the angle of the body's forward bend, is akin to the degree of intensity of the cyclist. An upright 90-degree posture is probably the most neutral cycling position, with head, shoulders, arms and hands at ease – as long as the saddle is comfortable as it supports most of the rider's weight. A mid-range 60- to 45-degree bend places a bit more weight on the shoulders and arms, but is also a relatively neutral position.

▶ Cyclists are very aware of small changes in body position and how these changes affect comfort and performance.

Most positions on a bike use the most powerful muscles of the body, those in the legs, buttocks and

lower back. While the upper body and arms get a good share of exercise, the abdominal muscles get the least work; therefore, supplemental core workouts are recommended to keep up with the legs.

It's usually the fatigue of longer rides that creates strains, like lower back pain, stiffness and aching around the neck and between the shoulders. The 45-degree 'flat back' position puts more strain on neck, shoulders, arms, wrists and hands, mainly because this position is adapted for more physically active cycling. No matter what degree of bend, it's best to keep a correct balance of weight and posture that allows full control of the bike.

Debunking KOPS

One of the traditional methods of bicycle fitting is setting the fore-aft saddle position based on the knee over the pedal spindle, known as KOPS. This method makes no sense for fitting recumbent bikes and has been somewhat debunked by frame builder and design engineer Keith Bontrager. He says the basis for KOPS is only a coincidental relationship, with weak statistical basis and no physiological bio-mechanical significance. Instead of looking at the thigh as pushing down on the pedals through the knee, it's better to consider the leg's attachment to the pedal and crank as a system of levers and pivots with pedal forces and joint torques. And to start a bike fitting with a cyclist's centre of gravity in an out-of-saddle climbing position.

Pedalling consists of a bio-mechanical lever system with five rigid elements (thigh, shin, foot, crank, seat tube) and five fulcrums (hip, knee, ankle, pedal, bottom bracket). A rider uses a variety of positions, including different out-of-saddle positions, for sprinting, climbing or bunny hopping, and the rider's centre of gravity moves around as the cyclist changes posture. The limbs and torso sometimes have to resist large force being applied to the pedals, and that force changes for each position. A good overall bike position has the cyclist well balanced, with weight distribution of 45% on the front wheel and 55% on the rear wheel, without having to expend excess muscular energy in arms and shoulders to support his or her weight.

4

Makes &
Manufacturers

Who makes what?

The makes and manufacturers of bicycles, frames,
components, accessories, wheels and tyres range
in size from multinational corporations to tiny
independents, and are comprised of industrialists,
investors, designers, engineers, marketers, inventors,
fabricators and bike riders who share a passion, a
special understanding and an obsession for bicycles.

For good or bad, the market drives many innovations
in the bike industry. It's often debatable whether a
product is revolutionary or superfluous, whether
one wants or needs another tyre size, brake system
or widget. New products are usually revealed at
big trade shows, such as Eurobike in Germany or
Interbike in the US, where makers, distributors,
retailers and media do business. Some big brands
don't need a trade show when a private junket for
trade partners works better.

Naming bikes

Bikes are often named after the frame maker, which
may be an artisan, a small factory or large brand.
For an aspiring frame builder, one of the biggest
accomplishments and responsibilities is to have
new decals with his or her name or brand on the
headbadge and downtube of a new bike. It may be
Jane Doe Cycles, Rad Velo Bikes or a portmanteau

word that combines the bicycle in any language: *bici*, *cykel*, *fiets*, *rad*, *rijwiel*, *sepeda* or *vélo*, root of the original name velocipede.

Then the model is named. Oh so many monikers! Thankfully, there are enough model names, acronyms and numbers to capture every imagination. Along with maker and model name comes the component group. That is, you have descriptive names combining group and frame, like a 'Super Record C-50' which is a 'Campy-equipped Colnago,' or a XTR Di2 Hydro-disc on an S-Works Epic Carbon 29er.

▲ New models on display at the Berliner Fahrradschau trade fair.

It's normal for a bike's country of origin to be complicated, as a bike can have its design and production of frame and parts from other makers in different places. OEM makers (original equipment manufacturers) produce different bikes to a model specification for other maker brands to sell.

Some makers and individuals have assembled bikes with parts made from a single country, such as the all-French constructeur bikes of the 1940s and 50s, the all-Italian road bikes of the 1960s and 70s, and the all-Japanese keirin bikes of the 1980s and 90s. Having every part of a complete bike made from locally-made sources, however, is a difficult, costly and compromised challenge, because suitable raw materials and components are not available everywhere.

▼ The lengthily named S-Works Epic Carbon 29er.

Brand leaders

The brand leaders make bikes and components in
all popular and high-end models. They sell bikes
and parts on every continent of the globe and they
support racing teams for cycling's biggest events.
These companies have research and testing facilities,
and all the marketing, trademarks, patents, licensing
and buy-in contracts of a corporate manufacturer.
Many well-known bike brands are owned by larger
holding companies that have other bike brands in
their portfolio. Here is a list of the biggest:

Accell Group in the Netherlands owns:
Batavus, Koga Miyata, Lapierre (France), Mercier (France), Raleigh
(USA, UK) and van Nicholas.

Advanced Sports International in the US owns:
Fuji, SE, Breezer and Kestrel.

Cycle Europe AB in Sweden holds:
Bianchi (Italy), Gitane (France), Peugeot (France) and Puch (Austria).

Dorel Industries in Canada owns US brands:
Cannondale, GT, Mongoose, Pacific and Schwinn.

Pon Holdings BV in the Netherlands owns:
Cervélo (Canada), Focus (Germany), Gazelle and Univega.

Selle Royal SpA in Italy owns:
Brooks (England), Crank Brothers (US), fi'zi:k, and Lookin.

Giant

Giant is considered the world's largest bicycle manufacturer, because it makes bikes for other major brands, as well as making all kinds of bikes under its own brand. Giant Manufacturing Co Ltd is a publicly traded company founded in 1972 in Dajia, Taichung, Taiwan, by King Lui. The firm entered into the OEM market, making bikes for Schwinn when their Chicago plant closed. It eventually established its own brand and expanded with Giant Europe in the Netherlands.

Being a huge maker of all kinds of different types of bike, Giant has come out with many innovative designs. One of those is the sloping road bike frame, known as Compact Road, with a top tube that slopes down towards the rear and has a smaller and tighter rear triangle, for a bit more stiffness and weight savings. Bike designer Mike Burrows brought many innovations to Giant, such as TCR composite road bikes, the Halfway folding bike, and the MCR monocoque time-trial bike.

▼ Giant Halfway folding bike.

Specialized

WWW.SPECIALIZED.COM

Mike Sinyard has built this California brand into a world leader. He founded Specialized in 1974, as a distributor of Campagnolo and Cinelli brands, visiting Bay Area retailers with his bike and trailer. He turned to Japan for making components and frames, and later to Taiwan and China for making a complete line of bicycle products, including bikes, parts, accessories and apparel. He's known for taking midday rides with his staff, including designers, engineers, marketers, lawyers and bike racers.

Specialized is credited with making the first mass-produced mountain bike, the Stumpjumper, based on an original design by Tom Ritchey. It is still being produced in different versions. The same is true of the Allez bike, one of their first road bikes, which also remains in their line. Their fancy Globe line of urban bikes has wobbled in and out of production, but their latest S-Works bikes are a hit, with the women's Amira, the men's Tarmac, the rough-road Roubaix, the TT Shiv and the sprinty Venge, designed with high-performance auto-maker McLaren.

The company has sponsored many racing teams and riders in various fields of cycling, from the legendary mountain biker Ned Overend to the Tour de France champion Alberto Contador. Their motto, 'Innovate or die' explains why Specialized remains at the top of the field.

Trek
WWW.TREKBIKES.COM

Trek is the big brand with the best name, because every ride is a good ride. Trek is more than its name, because it has owned other brands, such as Bontrager, Diamant (Germany), Electra, Gary Fisher, LeMond, Klein, and Villiger (Switzerland). Founded in 1976 in Waterloo, Wisconsin, by Richard Burke and Bevil Hogg, Trek began making quality lugged-steel framesets and eventually complete bikes that were as nice as those from Japan or Italy. Through the 1980s, the company expanded its offerings and reach, with a bonded aluminium frame model 2000, a bonded carbon composite frame model 2500, the entry-level Jazz line, the Trek Components Group (TCG) and Trek Wear, with subsidiaries in the UK and Germany.

Along with its popular hybrid bikes, Trek invested in moulded monocoque carbon composite manufacturing, producing its Optimum Compaction Low Void (OCLV) series of frames, with the early models 5500 and 5200, now the Madone, Domane and Émonda road bikes. Their full-suspension Y bike and time-trial Y-foil bike had moulded Y-shaped frames without seat tube. Trek's form of innovation included the Advanced Concepts Group (ACG) for tech developments, the Women's Specific Design (WSD) and Project One for customization of components and finish.

Brand leaders always have wins and losses, highlights and hard times. Trek benefited from the Lance Armstrong effect, when new cyclists obsessed by the cancer-surviving Trek-riding Tour de France champion bought more bikes. But Trek was hurt when America's other Tour champ, Greg LeMond, publicly questioned Armstrong's clean image, and Trek chose to fully support Armstrong, at the expense of their LeMond brand, until Armstrong's sports doping fraud became official.

▲ Trek Madone 2.1 H2 Compact Road Bike.

Historic brands

Several well-known bicycle brands date back to the nineteenth century. These historic makes expanded production enormously in the twentieth century, to survive in another life in the twenty-first. Some will say a historic or classic brand loses its soul when the founders pass on, when the name is sold or when the bikes become mass-produced, but these changes need not be a total loss. Some classic brands have been revived by passionate entrepreneurs who are attentive to authenticity and the brand's heritage, attempting faithful reproductions of the original make and models. Thanks to the dedication of these enthusiasts, the brands live on.

▼ A catalogue cover for Raleigh Bicycles, 1898.

Bianchi
WWW.BIANCHI.COM

Bianchi (pronounced bee-AHN-kee) is the world's oldest bicycle manufacturing company still in existence. It was founded in 1885, in the workshop of 21-year-old orphan Edoardo Bianchi at 7 via Nirone, in Milan, Italy, at a time when safety bicycles were becoming more popular than high-wheelers. Bianchi was the first in Italy to apply Dunlop's air-filled pneumatic tyres. He gave cycling lessons to Queen Margherita at the Royal Villa in Monza, riding a Bianchi with a crystal chain guard. The company expanded rapidly at the turn of the twentieth century, embracing all forms of industrial mechanization and producing a complete line of bicycles, motociclette, racing motorcycles, luxury sedans, trucks and buses.

Today's Bianchi bikes include various road, cross, time-trial, mountain, urban fixed-gear, city-trekking and vintage models, such as the Dama Bianca range for women and the L'Eroica special edition model.

Bianchi is best known for the colour of its Celeste bikes (pronounced che-les-te). A shade of pale green with tints of blue, it's known as Bianchi green, the colour of the sky in Milan, or a mixture of surplus military paint. Celeste usually appears on the high end models and it changes slightly from bike to bike over time. Along with the colour, Bianchi has always been associated with its bike-racing legends, from Costante Girardengo to Fausto Coppi, Felice Gimondi to Marco Pantani.

Cinelli
WWW.CINELLI.IT

Cinelli is one of the most famous names in bikes and cycling. Cino Cinelli founded his company in 1948, after a successful professional road-racing career with Bianchi and Frejus teams, winning the Giro di Lombardia and Milan-San Remo before World War II. The technical failures of the equipment he used became his new calling, and although his brother Giotto was making steel stems and handlebars in Florence, Cino moved the business to Milan, the centre of the Italian bicycle industry at the time. His Swiss wife, Hedi Matter, spoke several languages and was responsible for their success with foreign clients.

Some of Cinelli's innovations were too good to be true, such as the Bivalent hub system with interchangeable front and rear wheels and the M71

▼ Cinelli's
Laser Mia.

pedal cleat system with mechanical release. The
Super Corsa road frame, with Columbus tubes,
sloping fork crown and its distinctive fastback seat
clamp became an icon of classic bikes.

Cinelli was revived by Antonio Colombo, who took
over in 1978, as part of a series of company mergers
in which Cinelli became a division of Gruppo Srl.
The brand has since combined art, design and a
passion for beautiful bikes into traditional, innovative
and exotic styles, such as the Laser bicycle in all
its iterations, the Mario Cipollini playboy stems,
the UCI-banned Spinaci bars, and the CMX Cinelli
BMX frame.

Gazelle
WWW.GAZELLEBIKES.COM

Royal Dutch Gazelle is the famous bicycle brand
of the Netherlands, best known for its traditional
roadster bicycle. The company was founded in 1892
by Willem Kölling and Rudolf Arentsen, in Dieren,
the Netherlands, as a two-man operation in the
bicycle trade. Their first Gazelle bike production
began in 1902. With Dutch ties in the East Indies,
Gazelle exported many bikes, particularly to
Indonesia. In the 1960s, a race-bike workshop was set
up to make lightweight hand-built frames for racing
cyclists and the teams they sponsored.

It took 62 years to mark their first million bikes sold, when Gazelle became a public company. The second million came 12 years later in 1966, and the ten millionth bike was finished by Prince Willem Alexander in April of 1999. The official Royal title was awarded in 1992, in their centenary celebrations. Today, there are 450 employees making 300,000 bikes a year at the factory in Dieren.

The Gazelle Tour Populair roadster, in both Oma (ladies) and Opa (gents) formats, has all the practical features for reliable commuting: rod-lever brakes or drum, mudguards, mudflaps, skirt guards, chain cases, rear racks, elastic straps and dynamo lights.

Pashley
WWW.PASHLEY.CO.UK

A legendary maker of high-quality roadsters, carrier bikes and cargo tricycles, Pashley was founded in 1926 in Birmingham by William Rathbone Pashley. By the mid 1930s, the company became RW Pashley Ltd. and moved to Aston, where almost every component of their cycles was made in their own factory except the frame tubes and rubber tyres. William retired in the 1960s and his son, Dick, moved the company to new premises on Masons Road in Stratford-Upon-Avon. These days, Pashley's catalogue includes some 160 different models.

Pashley is best known for being one of the last of the
hand-built all-steel fully-equipped classic roadsters,
the Princess and Sovereign. They've made the
Royal Mail carrier cycles, the Moulton-licensed All
Purpose Bicycle (APB), the Land Rover-licensed XCB
mountain bikes, the Picador shopping trike and the
Classic 33 model of ice-cream vending trikes. For the
retro Guv'nor and Clubman bicycles, Reynolds 531
tubing was revived.

▲ The French
beauty brand
L'Occitane,
proudly displays
the iconic yellow
Pashley Delibike
outside a store.

Raleigh
WWW.RALEIGH.CO.UK

The heron is the symbol of Raleigh bicycles, which gained the distinction of having its products in more countries of the world than any other bike maker. The Raleigh story began in 1886, in the bicycle workshop of Woodhead, Angois and Ellis, on Raleigh Street, Nottingham, which made about three safety bikes a week. A local lawyer, Frank Bowden, bought one to help restore his health, and then bought the shop and founded the Raleigh Cycle Company in 1888.

Production grew rapidly and by 1896, the company had the world's largest bicycle factory, occupying three hectares, employing 850 workers and making about 30,000 bikes per year.

Raleigh was then bought by Tube Investments Group in 1960, which held Reynolds Tube Co, and the British Cycle Corporation, owners of Phillips Cycles, Hercules Cycle and Motor Co and eventually Carlton Cycles. Renamed Ti-Raleigh, the company underwent a series of territorial divisions, spin-offs, management buyouts, factory closings and ownership changes.

Along with traditional roadsters and sports bikes, like the DL-1 and Record Road Ace of 1939, Raleigh's notable models were the small-wheel bikes: RWS, Twenty and the super-cool Chopper of 1969. Top-of-the-line road bikes included the Professional, Competition and International models, all made with Reynolds 531 tubing.

Schwinn

WWW.SCHWINN.COM

Ignaz Schwinn founded this famous American brand in Chicago in 1895. He had immigrated to the US from Germany in 1891 and collaborated with compatriot meatpacking investor Adolph Arnold. Schwinn produced many seminal bikes during the era, now very collectible. With lower market share, executive complacency and rising costs and competition, the family business went bankrupt around 1980. Since then, Schwinn has continued to operate under various owners.

Schwinn's stable includes the high-end Paramount models, with track, road, touring and tandems dating from the late 1930s through the 1970s. The Black Phantom era was the balloon-tyre cruiser with chrome mudguards. The primordial ever-so-cool 1963 Sting-Ray with butterfly handlebars and banana seat became the fully equipped Apple Krate, Orange Krate, Lemon Krate and so on, with suspension, derailleurs and hand brakes.

Today the company shows glimpses of its former self, even though its place in the conglomerate of bike brands is as a mid-range producer, with classic Cruisers, the urban Coffee roadster, the Yahoo tandem and the Town and Country tricycle.

Velodromes

Velodromes are the cathedrals of cycling, where demi-god cyclists and their true believers gather to practise the sport in a venue that provides the ability to achieve peak performance in a measurable quantum. A sense of purity comes with riding a gracefully banked velodrome on a fixed-gear track bicycle.

Velodromes can be outdoor open-air tracks, semi-covered stadiums or indoor arenas and have surfaces of asphalt, concrete or various hardwoods. Some tracks are portable for temporary installation in different arenas. Most tracks range from 150 to 400 metres per lap, measured along the black pole line, which marks the bottom of the track. Olympic standard tracks are 250 metres, while traditional tracks are 333 metres. Tracks are homologated by the UCI according to their technical facilities and surface condition with categories 1 to 5.

Tracks are about five to nine metres wide. The markings begin with the 70 cm light blue band (or Côte d'Azur, where the Alps meet the Riviera), the flat inner lane, a neutral zone where riders enter and exit the racing zone. Racers inevitably dip below the black pole line, taking the whole track in sprints. To prevent short-cutting the pole line in timed races, foam blocks are placed around the turns. The pole position is the 70-cm-wide lane between the pole line and the red sprinters line. Once a sprinter commits to lead in the pole in the final 200 metres he or she must not stray out.

Other lane markings are the blue stayers line, which in Madison racing divides the race zone below from the rest zone above, where a black holding line marks the track's outer edge. The finish line crosses the home-straight with a 4 cm matte black line centred in a 72-cm-wide white band.

The Dunhill-sponsored velodrome, known as the Human-Powered Rollercoaster, broke from tradition at the 1995 Messenger Worlds in Toronto with a figure-eight design, where the crossing is on two levels. The super short and steep format of the Red Bull Minidromes, at about 25 metres in length, has also shown up in Tokyo, London, Vancouver, Paris and New York.

Race bikes

While there are other ways to prove a bicycle's quality, the racing scene is where bike makers and frame builders typically test and showcase their finest products. That is, by winning the Tour de France or a world championship, the best cyclist is supposed to be proof of a machine's competitive advantage and value.

In the classic history of road and track cycling, there are said to be the five Italian masters of the 1960s and 70s: Cino Cinelli, Ernesto Colnago, Faliero Masi,

Sante Pogliaghi and Ugo De Rosa. These makers raised the level of fabrication, crafting race-reliable machines, that were state-of-the-art for that period. Of course, that list leaves out many competent compatriots and colleagues, such as Mario Confente, Alfredo Gios, Giovanni Pelizzoli (Ciocc), Mario Rossin, Tiziano Zullo, Yoshi Konno (3Rensho) and Yoshiaki Nagasawa. There could just as well be five Benelux, British, French, Japanese and North American masters, all of whom raised the bar even higher in the 1970s and 80s.

Cannondale

WWW.CANNONDALE.COM

Named after a Metro-North station, Cannondale began in 1971 in Wilton, Connecticut, as a maker of backpacking and camping gear for cycle touring. In 1983, the company created its first frameset and bicycle (the ST-500) with a seamlessly joined oversize thin-wall aluminium tube frame and steel fork. Eventually, road, track and mountain bike models were offered, all made in their Pennsylvania factory.

Cannondale has innovated intuitive and exotic features, including the Cannondale Advanced Aluminum Design (CAAD) series of mountain and road frames; the Headshok suspension fork, with sets of needle bearings telescoping in the steering tube; and the unique Lefty fork, a monoblade disc-brake suspension set-up that provides ample mud clearance and tyre changes without wheel removal. Another Cannondale design is the BB30 bottom bracket standard with Hollowgram crankset – a stiff and lightweight combo.

Perhaps the company's worst idea was to launch into motorsports, with a line of motocross and all-terrain vehicles. They couldn't sell them for what they cost to make, leading the company to seek bankruptcy protection in 2003, at which point the bicycle division was purchased by Pegasus Capital Advisors. Since 2008, Cannondale has been a subsidiary of Dorel Industries sports and leisure division, with all manufacturing now in China and Taiwan.

▶ A Cannondale team out on a practice session for the Giro d'Italia in Belfast, Northern Ireland, in 2014.

Pinarello
WWW.PINARELLO.COM

Giovanni 'Nani' Pinarello founded Cicli Pinarello SpA. in 1952 in Treviso, Italy. This happened shortly after a winning the infamous Maglia Nera (Black Jersey) – the curiously contested prize for last place overall – in the 34th Giro d'Italia and riding a lap of honour in Milan's Vigorelli velodrome with champions Fiorenzo Magni and Louison Bobet.

With roots in racing, Pinarello began building competition road and track bikes – usually lugged steel frames with Columbus tubing and parts pantographed with the name or the Pinarello logo. The Montello SLX model of the 1980s is a highly regarded bike. Since the entry of Giovanni's son, Fausto Pinarello, into the family business, their bikes have continued the progression of aluminium, magnesium and carbon composite frame materials, with innovations such as the series of time-trial bikes, the Espada and Parigina, of the mid-1990s.

With their recent Team Sky sponsorship, Pinarello has collaborated with Jaguar, particularly on the Bolide time-trial bike, which features hidden brakes that are integrated into the forks and chainstays. Pinarello leads the modern peloton of bike makers with eleven Tour de France victories since 1988.

▲ Sir Bradley Wiggins' Pinarello bike during the Tour of Catalonia.

Colnago
WWW.COLNAGO.COM

An apprentice with Gloria bicycles since he was 13, Ernesto Colnago built his first frames and founded his company in 1952. While building frames, he served as race mechanic under Faliero Masi, and eventually became head mechanic for the Molteni team in 1963. A win in the 1970 Milan-San Remo classic (finishing by the San Remo casino) inspired Colnago to adopt his famous logo, the Asso di Fiori or Ace of Clubs. Once superstar Eddy Merckx joined Molteni, Colnago's reputation grew and he branched out into mass-production bikes.

Colnago introduced various shaped frame tubes, such as Oval CX and the crimped Gilco tubes found on the Master Pui. The Bititan titanium frame had two slender down tubes, instead of one standard size tube. His first monocoque carbon-fibre bike was a disc-wheel track bike prototype introduced in 1981. Collaborating with automaker Ferrari on carbon composites, he credits their engineers for inspiring the Precisa straight-blade steel fork of 1987.

Since 1994, after producing the flagship carbon frame called the C-40 (named after the number of years he had spent building bikes), Colnago has kept up-to-date with innovation, releasing the C-50 and more recently the C-60 – all made in Italy. Since 2006 many entry- and mid-level frames have been sourced from Taiwan. Ernesto maintains that design is the soul of his frames, no matter where they are made.

▲ A win in the Milan-San Remo classic inspired Colnago to adopt his famous logo, the Asso di Fiori or Ace of Clubs.

Cervélo

WWW.CERVELO.COM

Cervélo is a Canadian maker founded in Toronto in
1995 by Gerard Vroomen and Phil White, the name
being a mix of *cervello* ('brain' in Italian) and *vélo*.
They offer four styles of carbon race bikes: the classic
road R-series, the aero road S-series, the time-trial
P-series and track T-series, in addition to the Project
California series, handmade in Los Angeles. Their
newest features are the Squoval square-oval tube
shapes and future-proof cable management, ensuring
compatibility with new component systems.

▼ Cervélo R3
Road Bike.

Look Cycle

WWW.LOOKCYCLE.COM

Look Cycle International is a French company based in Nevers. Its logo and colours feature a Piet Mondrian inspired design, made famous in cycling by Tour de France champions Bernard Hinault and Greg LeMond. In the early 1980s they introduced a clipless pedal based on the ski bindings the company made since its start in 1951. This was followed by their first carbon bicycle frame, the KG 86, and their first monocoque composite frame, KG 196 in the early 1990s. The ski division was sold to Rossignol in 1994 and the bike division became Look Cycle. Their TT and track bikes have beautifully designed front ends, a near perfect integration of form and function.

Artisan makers

Many bicycle professionals will argue that the finest bikes are made by artisan builders, people who have the skill and obsession to get the details as perfect as possible. Words like 'bespoke', 'tailored', 'custom-fit' and 'made-to-measure' are associated with hand-built bicycles, and the demand for these products is on the rise. In the United States, there were fewer than 50 artisan builders working in 2010, and there were more than 200 in business in 2015.

Hand-built bicycle shows are the places to go in order to see the best of the best. These shows include the North American Hand-Built Show (NAHBS), Bespoked in the UK and others that are held in art and design centres.

Artisan makers include material specialists working in steel, stainless steel, aluminium, titanium, composites and wood. They have machine tools, frame jigs, heavy alignment tables and their flame of choice – a brazing torch or welding stick. Finishing includes frame prep and painting, applying enamel wet paint or an electrostatic powder coat, plating in chrome or nickel and, finally, the graphic details with pinstripes, decals and badges.

Herse
WWW.RENEHERSE.COM

René Herse specialized in handmade porteur, touring, randonneur and racing bicycles. In the late 1930s, Herse left the aircraft industry and began producing lightweight bicycle components, including stems, cranks, pedals and brakes. Frame production began around 1940 in Levallois, outside Paris, and Herse became one of the leading French 'constructeurs', making complete bicycles in-house.

With the successes that Herse designs experienced in the demanding French brevet and randonneur technical trials, they became known worldwide and his innovations were copied throughout the cycling industry. In 1976, René Herse passed away and his daughter, Lyli, a French National road and track champion, and his son-in-law, Jean Desbois, took

▼ René Herse Randonneuse 42/75 refurbished by Jim Langley.

over the company. While the occasional Herse part was still produced, the company ceased regular production in the 1980s. Around 2007, the family sold the rights and remaining material to Michael Kone in Boulder, Colorado, and now the René Herse brand and design carries on with bicycle fabrication by Mark Nobilette in nearby Longmont, Colorado, and component manufacturing licensed to Compass Bicycles in Seattle, Washington.

Dario Pegoretti
WWW.DARIO-PEGORETTI.COM

Italian frame builder Dario Pegoretti is the most artistically inspired finisher in the industry and his frames are his canvases, filled with collage, freehand brushwork and colourful designs. Most of his bikes are sport or competition bikes named after songs, though as the collectible value increases, these may more likely hang on a wall as art.

Pegoretti has produced more than 30,000 bicycles in steel and aluminium in his 40-year career. Apprenticing with his father-in-law, Luigino Milani, he made bikes for cycling stars such as Miguel Indurain, Marco Pantani and Floyd Landis, as well as for the actor Robin Williams. He pioneered the now common TIG-welded lugless frames and has collaborated with manufacturers in producing speciality tubing, such as Pego-Richie tubes made with Richard Sachs.

Coast Cycles

WWW.JOHNNYCOAST.COM

Before his tenth birthday, Johnny Coast had already started welding at his father's custom car and hot rod shop in Colorado. He was always messing with bikes as a youngster – tall bikes, choppers and racing machines – and after studying frame building at United Bicycle Institute in Oregon and the school of Koichi Yamaguchi in Colorado, Coast set up his own shop in 2004. The shop was known as his 'chicken hut' and sat at the end of a cul-de-sac in Bushwick, Brooklyn, New York.

Coast's motto is 'Hand-built, silver-brazed, quality frames: Beautiful, classic, true to the process.' He builds high-quality frames that will last a lifetime, using the same techniques that master builders have used for generations. He builds every frame himself, and every element bears incredible skill and craftmanship. One technique he uses when joining tubes is the fillet-brazed half lug 'bilaminate' construction, which combines the seamless look of filled in joints and the sleeved look of lugged joints.

Coast Cycles offers six hand-built silver-brazed frame styles: City, Mixte, Rando, Road, Touring and Track, as well as custom stems, racks and bag-holding decaleurs. Tubing selections include Columbus, True-Temper, Deda and Reynolds.

Brompton

WWW.BROMPTON.COM

Brompton is one of the most popular and practical folding bicycles, notable for its quick-fold, self-supporting compact size and numerous accessories. All models are based on a hand-made curved, hinged steel frame, with 16" (37-349) wheels, a pivoting rear triangle with suspension, a telescoping seat post and a collapsible handlebar.

▼ The Brompton folds down to a portable, practical size so it can be carried or easily taken on public transport.

The bike was designed in 1975–6 by Andrew Ritchie in his South Kensington flat overlooking the Brompton Oratory in London, England. With his first patent in 1977, low-volume ad-hoc production began in 1981, but it wasn't until 1988 that he received

enough backing to resume production in units under a railway arch in Brentwood. Ritchie has dedicated most of his working life to perfecting the bike, admittedly an obsession.

A Brompton is made to order by choosing between various features and options, including standard and superlight frame types, with titanium forks and rear frame, multiple colour options for frame and extremities, four handlebar types and gearing options with 1-, 2-, 3- or 6-speeds. One has the option of three kinds of tyres and seatpost heights, standard or firm suspension, mudguards, rack, easy wheels, a variety of purpose-built bags and battery or hub dynamo LED lighting.

Gearing: sprockets & ratios

Gear measures are meant to be simple, practical calculations – a way to communicate gear size among different bikes relative to cadence, speed, gradient and terrain. Yet differences and inaccuracies arise between imperial and metric users, and the fact that many wheel sizes are nominal and not actual accurate sizes.

Sprocket size is the easiest way to relate gear size on a chain-drive bicycle. Sprocket size is the number of teeth of the two sprockets, the front chainring and rear cog. A bike with a 45-tooth chainring and 18-tooth cog is said to have a '45 18', written as 45 x 18.

Gear ratio is the basis for other gear measures. It's the relative measure of crank to wheel rotation, as each turn of the crank results in a number of turns of the wheel. On a chain-drive bike the number of teeth on the front chainring are divided by the number of teeth on the rear cog. A 45-tooth chainring and 18-tooth cog, therefore, has a 2.50 gear ratio.

Gear inches is the formula commonly used by English speakers. It's a nominal measure of gear ratio times drive wheel diameter in inches. A standard 27" wheel bike with 45 x 18 sprocket combination or 2.50 gear ratio has 67.5 gear inches.

Development is the term for metric system users to define the distance travelled in one pedal rotation, measured as gear ratio times wheel circumference in metres. A bike with 45 x 18 sprockets or 2.50 gear ratio, and 700C wheels with 2.096 metre circumference has 5.24 metres development.

Gain ratio is a new measure, a pure ratio that calculates wheel radius divided by crank length times the gear ratio. It accounts for the leverage of gears on bikes with different wheel sizes and crank lengths. A road bike with 700C wheels (340 mm radius), 170 mm length cranks, and a 45 x 18 sprocket combination (2.50 gear ratio) has a gain ratio of 5.00.

Gear charts have been a handy guide to select gear combinations by showing virtually every sprocket and cog size, defined as gear ratios, gear inches or metres development, for a given tyre and wheel size. A specific gear chart is a table of gear combinations for a given bike, with two or three columns for front sprockets and as many rows as rear cogs. These notes were attached with clear tape to the stem or top tube of the bike, now a gear chart can appear in the same place on a phone screen or power meter cycle computer.

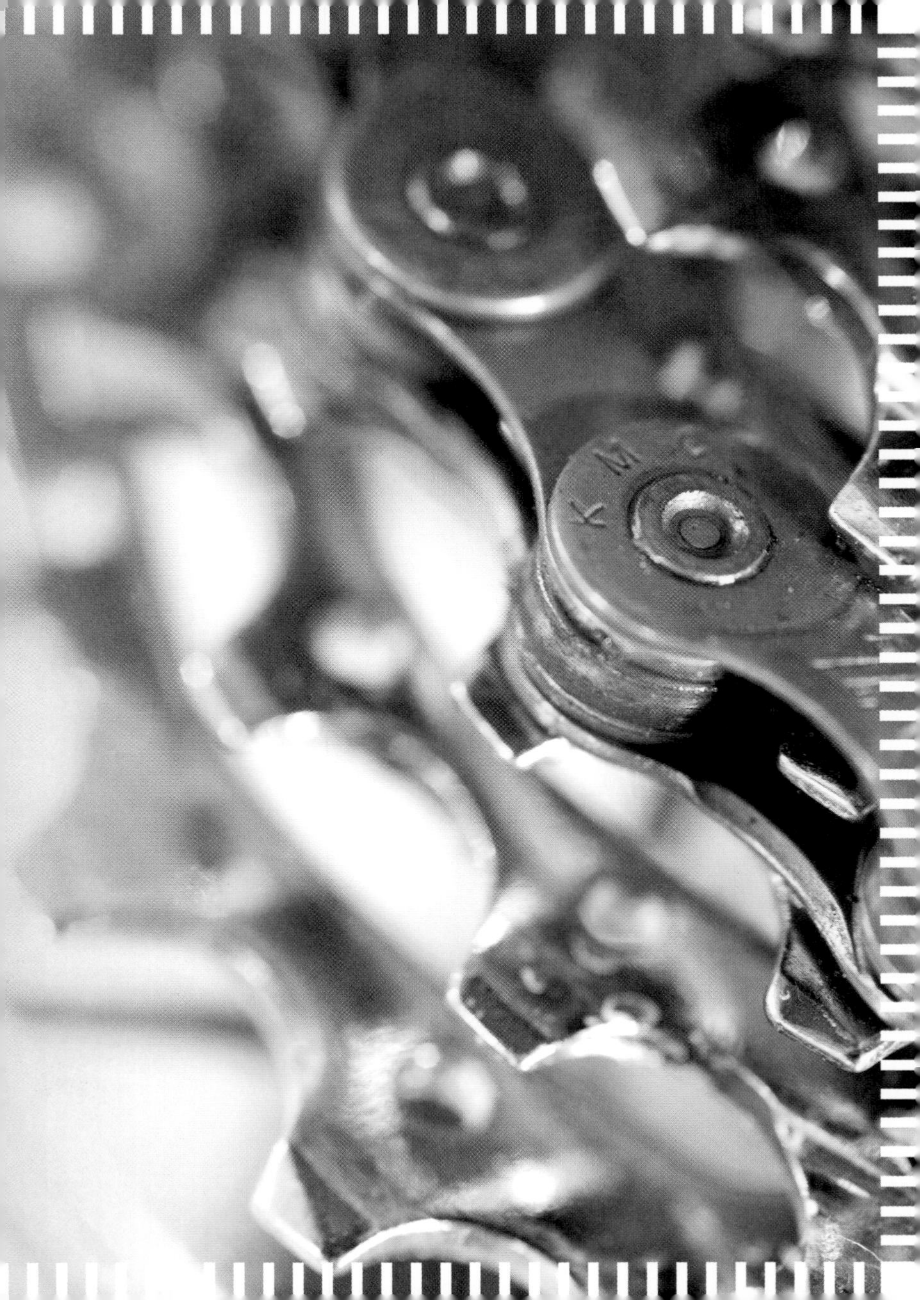

Component makers

A bicycle is the sum of its parts – and even the finest frames can still benefit from some tricked-up add ons. Whether it's a hand-stitched saddle or a bespoke chain set, there is a world of artisan components to entrance the truly bicycle-obsessed.

Brooks England
WWW.BROOKSENGLAND.COM

Brooks England stands out among the world's leather saddle makers for being both old school with its original machinery and factory process, yet very chic and hip with a quality and style that has remained fashionable for well over a century.

JB Brooks & Co was founded in 1866 by John Boultbee Brooks, a leatherworker of horse tack, in Birmingham. According to legend, after his horse died in 1878 he borrowed a bicycle and found the seat too hard so he made one of his own in leather. Brooks filed his first saddle patent in 1882 and introduced the Climax saddle in 1890, as well as various saddlebags and other leather goods for cyclists. In the 1950s the company invested in purpose-built saddle-making machinery that's still in use. After the company was bought by Raleigh around 1960, the factory moved to Smethwick.

The B17 saddle was introduced some time between 1879 and 1898. Although the exact year of creation isn't known, it's one of the oldest bicycle parts still in production because of its comfort and popularity. Its width has varied, from 21.5 cm (8½ in) in the early years to 17 cm (6¾ in) in a current Standard model.

▼ A classic Brooks leather saddle.

Campagnolo

WWW.CAMPAGNOLO.COM

Campagnolo has produced some of the finest-quality bicycle components for more than 80 years, making it one of the most revered brands in cycling. The company grew large enough in the 1960s to make sports car wheels, scooter brakes and satellite chassis, but returned to its cycling roots in its second generation.

The Campagnolo story began in November 1927, when Tullio Campagnolo was alone at the front of a race, preparing to climb the Croce d'Aune pass in freezing conditions. His hands were so numb, however, that he could not loosen the wing nuts to disengage the wheel and shift to a lower gear. That incident inspired him to redesign the lever to make it quick-release, which he patented in 1930 and began producing in 1933. That same year he

▼ A Vintage Campagnolo chain set and Regina Oro gold block and chain.

founded his company, SpA Brevetti Internazionali Campagnolo, in a back room of his father's hardware store in Vicenza, Italy.

Campagnolo's innovative products were the parallelogram derailleurs, from Grand Sport, to Record, Nuovo Record and Super Record, and the brakes, from Record side-pull calipers to Delta parallelogram linkage calipers and Super Record dual pivot calipers. Campagnolo's hub and crank bearings were the smoothest around, yet track racers would replace grease with oil to reduce resistance and ease spin. When Tullio died in 1983, the same year a special 50th anniversary edition groupset was made, his son Valentino took the helm of the company. The latest innovations are the ever-improving Ergo brake-gear levers, the Ultra-Torque crankset with Hirth couplings, the EPS electronic drivetrains and a new 80th anniversary 11-speed group.

In the heyday of vintage Campagnolo, the brand took on an iconic nature. People spoke of a bicycle being '100 per cent Campagnolo,' or 'all-Campy', which was impossible because the company didn't make frames, tyres or saddles (until 1992). Anything awesome would be described as 'tutto Campagnolo'. Cyclists using inferior components would 'cramp-and-go-slow,' unlike those using Campagnolo. Other competing brands such as Zeus, Simplex and Huret were described as 'Campy replicas', that performed 'like Campy at half the price'.

Reynolds

WWW.REYNOLDSTECHNOLOGY.BIZ

Reynolds was founded in 1898 in Birmingham, England, as the Patented Butted Tube Company, making tubing exclusively for bicycles, based on the patent by Alfred Milward Reynolds and Thomas Hewitt. Demand expanded during the 1890s and even more with the advent of motor vehicles and aircraft in the early twentieth century. By 1928 the company at Hay Hall was renamed Reynolds Tube Company Ltd, when their best tubing was named HM for its high manganese and low molybdenum content, and dubbed as 'Her Majesty'.

Throughout the classic period of lightweight road bicycles, from the mid-1930s to late 1980s, Reynolds was best known for its 531 tubing ('five-three-one'), which refers to its alloy ratio of manganese and molybdenum. Some twenty million framesets had 531 tubing by the company's 50th anniversary, and the Reynolds' 27 Tour de France victories on bike frames made with their tubular materials technology.

Besides limited editions of 531, Reynolds now offers tubing in two stainless-steel models, three air-hardening or heat-treated seamless steels, two cold-worked, chrome-moly models, two grades of aluminium alloy and two alloys of titanium.

Shimano
WWW.SHIMANO.COM

Shimano Iron Works, founded by Shozaburo Shimano, originally made casting reels for fly-rod fishing and began making bicycle freewheels in 1921. After Shozaburo's death in 1958, his sons Shozo, Keizo and Yoshizo grew the company, particularly in Europe and the Americas.

Among Shimano's innovations are the freehub system of splined cassettes (which replaced freewheels), the Shimano Index System (SIS) – that familiar click stop that precisely shifts to each gear – and the Shimano Total Integration (STI) and Dual Control, with integrated gear and brake levers. 'Shimano Pedaling Dynamics' (SPD) is a widely used system of pedals, cleats and shoes, with two-bolt recessed cleats that are far better for walking than typical three-bolt road cleats.

Shimano's top-shelf groups are Dura-Ace for road bikes, XTR for mountain bikes, and DXR for BMX bikes. Their Nexus and Nexave systems, consisting of internally geared hubs, shifters and brakes, are designed for comfort and commuting bikes.

Shimano's latest innovation, introduced in 2009, is the Dura-Ace Di2 (digital integration intelligence) electronic gear-shifting system. It includes solid-state switches, a lithium-ion battery pack and motorized derailleurs with worm gears. It costs and weighs a bit more than the mechanical Dura-Ace, but functions more easily.

SRAM
WWW.SRAM.COM

Chicago-based SRAM is a privately held corporation that was founded in 1987. The name is an acronym of its founders, Scott, Ray and Sam, with Ray being the middle name of company CEO Stan Day. Their first product was Grip Shift, a popular twist-grip gear shifter. Seeking a share of the OEM market with big bike makers and a fair playing field, SRAM successfully sued Shimano in 1990. Through a series of acquisitions aimed at global domination, their marquis brands include Sachs internal gear hubs, RockShox suspension forks, Avid brakes, Truvativ components, Quarq power meters and Zipp carbon wheels, cranks, handlebars and stems.

SRAM has about eighteen groupsets for road and off-road bikes, with the highest quality being Red group for road bikes and XX1 and XO1 for off-road bikes. One of their proprietary features is the SRAM 1:1 Exact Actuation™ cable pull ratio. It works well only when paired with SRAM shifters and derailleurs, making these parts incompatible with other brands.

SRAM 1x™ components, introduced first for off-road bikes (but now available for road use as Force1), have a single chainwheel that has teeth designed not to shift off, a roller bearing clutch rear derailleur, and Mini Cluster™ 11-speed cassette with a 10 through 42 teeth spread. It's amazing that this system began with mountain bikes, since keeping the chain on a

bike with a single front sprocket and multi-speed
rear cogs has usually required extra chain keepers
or tensioners.

SRAM's innovations for road bikes include the
DoubleTap gear lever, the Red HydroR hydraulic
rim and disc brakes and Red eTap wireless electronic
shifting system, with a battery in each derailleur
instead of a single battery pack.

▼ SRAM brake
levers on a
racing bicycle's
dropped
handlebars.

Flat fix: patch, boot, liner & sealant

You can only avoid flats by riding attentively and following the smoothest path without debris and potholes, keeping tyres inflated at the recommended pressure, using a stable rim strip and tyre liner and the thickest belted tyres with a thorn-proof tube. Even then you need also to be carrying some good karma.

Everything about bikes can be complicated and they do not get easier to fix the more wear they endure. Replacing a worn-out tyre or tube requires removing and replacing a wheel and can involve complications such as frozen or stripped axle nuts, duct-taped, hosed-clamped quick releases or a stuck-through axle with a vice-grip and hammer nightmare.

Fixing a flat requires finding the cause. The reason for a typical flat tyre can be discussed at length, but there is almost always an innocuous explanation. Most likely the tube was punctured through the tyre by a sharp piece of glass, wire or a thorn. Sometimes it's still in the tyre, and needs to be removed before it does more damage. Another cause of a flat is when misaligned brake pads rub a tear in the tyre casing, which makes the tube explode. Pinch flats, or snake bites, occur when bottoming out on

the rim because of too soft tyres with low air pressure. There's a huge amount of tube pinching while reinstalling narrow tyres on deep rims in the realm of fixie bikes. Problems also occur when rim strips travel away from spoke holes or push into the rim bead seat.

Every day your tubes are losing air because they are slightly porous. High-pressure tyres (over 100 psi) need re-inflating every day for tubulars or every week for clinchers. Regular tyres and tubes go soft in a month or two. Tubes filled with CO_2 lose pressure faster than air-filled tubes, and latex tubes lose air within hours but provide the best performance because the rubber is more supple than butyl tubes. Some tubes come with a sealant to plug up holes. Tubes with removable valve cores can be filled with tyre sealant. Sometimes when a sealant-filled tyre gets punctured, the sealant sprays out as the wheel goes round, making a sticky mess. When you 'catch a flat' on a tubular, you either change the tyre or, in a race, the wheel because it's quicker and safer. To change the tyre you tear off the glued carcass from the rim and stretch a slightly pre-glued new or patched spare tyre on the rim.

▶ A good puncture repair kit is an essential piece of kit for all cyclists.

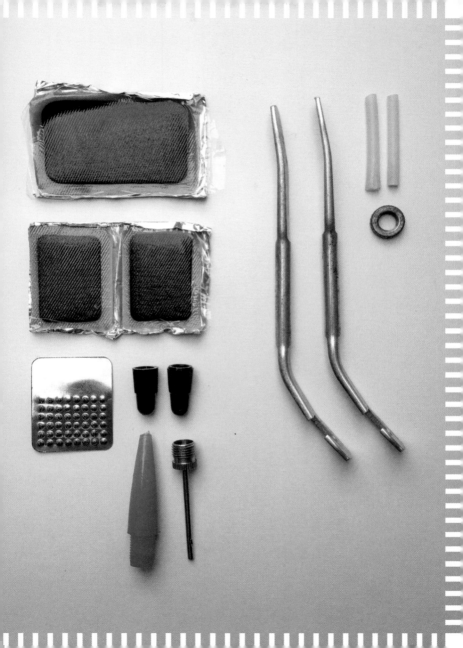

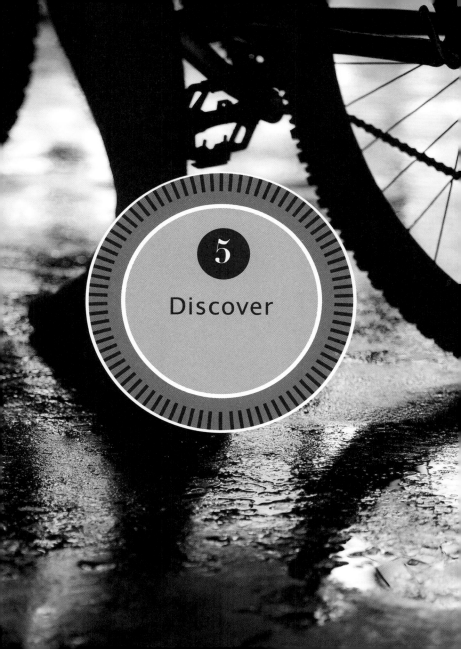

5

Discover

Bicycle culture

Bicycle culture is expressed in the diversity of its beautiful machines, the daily health-giving commute, the challenge of a big ride and the lively, social nature of cyclists. When one becomes enamoured by bikes and cycling, it's often the social, physical and aesthetic aspects that bring the most pleasurable and memorable feelings. There's an international appeal for this popular vehicle that transcends borders and politics and unites languages and cultures.

Cycling is a big part of global tourism; millions of people travel to scenic places and bike-related events throughout the world. Travelling on a bicycle – being open to the surrounding landscape, moving at a variety of speeds, flying downhill or stopping to smell the flowers – brings an appreciation for a place and the feeling of being in the moment.

Big rides & tours

Big bike events can attract tens of thousands of participants coming from both near and far for sightseeing and cycling camaraderie. These rides offer both short and long distances, typically 40, 80, 125 or 200 kilometres.

The Big Apple, New York City, has the Five Boro Bike Tour hosted by Bike New York. It's a 67.5-km, all-day extravaganza over highways, byways and bridges through Manhattan, Queens, the Bronx, Brooklyn and Staten Island. Every kind of bike – cargo, recumbent, fixie, unicycle, high wheel, freeride, time trial – can be seen along the route.

Montreal's Tour de l'Île is considered the largest annual cycling event in the world, with 30,000 to 45,000 participants riding either the classic 50-km route, a short 28-km route or a round-the-island 100-km route. It began with a group ride to celebrate International Bicycle Day, which is held the first weekend of each June. Advocate Bob Silverman coined the slogan 'Vive la vélorution', which inspired Vélo Québec to organize a gathering for cyclists of all ages to demonstrate to the authorities just how popular cycling was becoming.

▼ 31st Annual Five Boro Bike Tour, in which 30,000 cyclists peddled 67 km on car-free streets through the five boroughs of New York City.

RideLondon is a popular two-day festival of cycling in July, a legacy of the 2012 Olympics. The festival includes the RideLondon Cycling Show, the FreeCycle family ride, the 24-km Handcycle Classic, the Grand Prix evening criterium races, and the Surrey-100 sportive ride that precedes the Surrey Classic, a 200-km professional race.

The annual Étape du Tour is the amateur cyclist's chance to ride a stage of the Tour de France on the same route as the professional race. It's held by the Tour de France organizer ASO. Cyclists can register through select bike-tour guide companies. It often features the Queen stage, the most demanding part of the race. Spectating at the three-week races such as the Tour de France and Giro d'Italia is way more exciting than watching the racing on TV, by riding parts of the route, lining the barriers for a time trial or camping on sides of mountains with the *tifosi* (excitable fans) running along as the race passes by.

For those who like the mountains, there are rides such as La Marmotte, the Maratona Dolomite, the Trans Continental route from the Atlantic Ocean to the Mediterranean Sea across the Pyrenees and the Haute Route rides – which include the Alps, Pyrenees and Dolomites. There's also the Cape Town Cycle Tour, or Cape Classic, held in March in South Africa, and the Tour of the California Alps (also known as the Markleeville Death Ride).

Gran Fondo-style rides are a new trend. They are semi-competitive events held on scenic routes between 100 and 225 km in length, and often feature celebrity riders, plentiful feed stations, tech support and swag bags. The Gran Fondo is an Italian tradition, blending a challenging sporting event with a cultural experience. They're named after almost all the big names of cycling. More than a typical charity ride, Gran Fondos have starting groups of participants based on ranking from pro to tourist, with timing chips, medals for participants, artisanal food and beverages, souvenir jerseys and, sadly, route cheaters and trained dopers. A few Fondos require cyclists to wear the same design of jersey, which takes away the sea of colourful jerseys – some from rides and groups from far-away places – often seen on most big rides.

Another trend is the vintage or retro gathering, for which the bikes, equipment and attire of a certain era are rolled out. Most vintage rides are local gatherings of people who appreciate the various historic or classic periods of cycling. The Eroica (meaning 'heroic') rides are the biggest of this type, established in 1997 in Tuscany to preserve the heritage of the white gravel roads and the romantic idea of a heroic way of cycling, where 'hunters of feelings and emotions pursue a sustainable lifestyle of pure clean cycling', 'indicating the future by looking to the past'. The original L'Eroica in Gaiole has now spread to Eroica Japan (picture Mount Fuji's black volcanic gravel roads), Eroica Britannia in the Peak District, Eroica Hispania in the Spanish province of La Rioja, Eroica California in Paso Robles and Eroica Primavera, which takes place south of Siena in Tuscany, Italy.

Local community

Local sources are often the best places to find everything cycling. Bike magazines often rate towns as 'bicycle friendly', which are usually those with the best facilities and infrastructure, as well as active, enthusiastic cyclists and political and social support.

Around 1980, a series of bicycle planning conferences in Europe and North America led to the growth of advocacy organizations that represent local, regional, national, continental and international communities of cyclists. What began as Velo Mondial meetings in Montreal (1996), Amsterdam (2000) and Cape Town (2006), turned into annual Velo-City global conferences that showcase the best policies, promotion and provisions for bikes and cycling. The results of these conferences are better infrastructure, city bike programmes, greenways and cross-border bike routes.

Alley cats, messenger races and critical mass rides tend to combine civic and worker pride with civil disobedience, since they can take place on busy streets congested with traffic. For those looking for something a little less stressful, midnight rides are a nice way for groups to enjoy nightlife on dark trails, or to avoid traffic on usually busy city streets. Many rides are based around fashion, such as the Tweed Rides (held in most big cities), the 'formal wear' Brompton Rides and the Saturday Style Ride in Zurich.

▶ A bike covered with umbrellas in the Bike Parade during the Velo-city congress of urban cycling in Nantes, France, 2015.

The World Naked Bike Ride is similar but with the opposite take. Another expression of bike culture are the Demolition Derby, Bike Toss and Bike Kill events, where 'mutant' bikes are celebrated and then destroyed by merry-making bike fanatics.

Bikes and cycling haven't escaped the popular art form of cinema and movies. The Bicycle Film Festival is held annually in New York at the Anthology Film Archives, and screens feature-length films and independent shorts. The International Cycling Film Festival has been held in Germany and Poland since 2006. Both these events include art shows, street fairs, acrobatic and freestyle shows and after parties.

Exhibits & museums

Bicycle enthusiasts can discover more at various museums, halls of fame and makers' showrooms. Museums that focus on bike technology and innovation – such as the National Cycle Museum in Llandrindod Wells, UK; Nijmegen Velorama in the Netherlands; and the Bicycle Museum Cycle Center in Sakai, Japan – have historic bikes on show, interactive displays and education programmes.

There are several halls of fame related to cycling and racing, such as the Centrum Ronde van Vlaanderen in Belgium; the Marin Museum of Bicycling and Mountain Bike Hall of Fame in Fairfax, California; and the cathedral of the patron saint of cycling,

Madonna del Ghisallo, which sits above Lake Como in Italy, along the route of the Tour of Lombardia. Inside are bikes, jerseys, pennants, portraits and trophies. Outside stands a sculpture showing the balance of cycling.

A maker's showroom can be anything from the intimate shop of a custom frame builder to the exhibit space of a major brand. The bikes on display tend to show the beginnings, highlights and, perhaps, a rarity bicycle.

▼ The cathedral of the patron saint of cycling, Madonna del Ghisallo, Italy.

Useful contacts

Each kind of bicycle has its own following, and you can start fuelling your own obsession by searching online and finding enthusiast blogs or forums, where aficionados discuss bike topics, track auction items and dispel bike myths and urban legends.

Opposite are just a few websites for events, societies and groups to get you started.

Five Boro Bike Tour
www.bike.nyc

Tour de l'Île Montréal
www.velo.qc.ca

RideLondon
www.ridelondon.co.uk

L'Étape du Tour
www.letapedutour.com

L'Eroica Gaiole
www.eroicagaiole.com

Eroica Rides
www.eroica.cc

Gourmet Century
www.gourmetcentury.com

**Adventure Cycling
Association**
www.adventurecycling.org

National Cycle Museum
www.cyclemuseum.org.uk

**Nationaal Fietsmuseum
Velorama Nijmegen**
www.velorama.nl

**Bicycle Museum Cycle
Center**
www.bikemuse.jp

Tour of Flanders Centre
www.crvv.be

Bicycle Film Festival
www.bicyclefilmfestival.com

**International Cycling
Film Festival**
www.cyclingfilms.de

**Union Cycliste
International (UCI)**
www.uci.ch

**International Human-
Powered Vehicle
Association (IHPVA)**
www.ihpva.org

**European Cyclists'
Federation**
www.ecf.com

**International Mountain
Bicycling Association**
www.imba.com

Cyclists' Touring Club (CTC)
www.ctc.org.uk

Glossary

Aerobic Exercise in which the amount of muscular effort allows oxygen replenishment by comfortable breathing.

Alloy A blend of metals. Often refers to aluminium alloy, as opposed to other metal or plastic materials. *See also* Chromoly.

Anaerobic High-intensity exercise in which the amount of muscular effort quickly exceeds the ability to replenish oxygen by rapid breathing.

Anatomic An item specifically designed to accommodate the shape of the body, such as anatomic handlebar grips or anatomic seats.

Axle A solid or hollow shaft that is the central fitting in a rotating mechanism, such as in a bottom bracket, hub, or pedal.

Bell lap A lap in a circuit or track race, in which a bell is rung at the finish line to announce that there is one lap to go.

Berm In off-road terrain, a curved embankment that allows more speed and traction than a flat corner.

Bottom Bracket The axle and bearing assembly which the pedal cranks are attached to, and which fit inside the bottom bracket shell of a bike frame. Often abbreviated to BB.

Brifter A combined brake and gear lever component.

Bunny-hop To jump over an obstacle by lifting the wheels, either simultaneously, or the front wheel followed by the rear wheel.

Cadence The rate of pedalling, measured as number of revolutions per minute (RPM). A typical cadence can range from 30 to 120 RPM; a very high cadence is over 200 RPM.

Century An organized group ride, the route distance being approximately 100 kilometres (62 miles) or 100 miles (124 kilometres).

Chromoly (also Chro-mo or Chrome-molybdenum) An alloy of steel commonly used in good-quality bike frames and components.

Clunker A bike used for casual riding, typically a single-speed cruiser. Also, Klunker, or as a verb, clunking, klunking.

Cluster The set of cogs or sprockets on a multi-speed cassette or freewheel. A cluster with only one tooth difference per cog is called a straight block or corncob.

Compact A compact bike frame has a sloping top tube designed to be lighter and easier than a standard horizontal top tube bike. A compact crankset has double chainwheels that are smaller in size than a standard racing double, offering gear ratios more like a standard triple chainwheel crankset.

Criterium (also Crit) A circuit race, consisting of many laps on a short course, usually held on city streets.

Detangler A special brake cable fitting that allows the handlebars to spin a full 360-degrees.

Dish/Dishing The dish-like shape of a wheel's spokes laced from the hub to the rim. Most front wheels have a symmetric dish, while most rear multi-speed cassette or freewheel wheels have an offset dish with the drive side flatter than the non-drive side.

Drafting The energy-saving position of a bike rider following closely behind another rider, in the draft or slipstream of the lead rider breaking into the wind.

Echelon A group of cyclists in a drafting formation, in a diagonal paceline, that is staggered across the road because of a crosswind.

Ergometer An indoor stationary bike with a power meter for training or fitness testing.

Lugs Metal sleeve-like fitting that holds tubes in a joint.

Monocoque A method of bike frame construction in which the outer layer, skin or shell provides structural support and load bearing function. Most moulded carbon fibre frames have monocoque construction.

Motor-pacing A training technique and race format, on road or track, in which cyclists are paced by a moped or motorcycle.

Musette A small sack with a single shoulder strap used to carry bottles and food.

Omnium A multi-discipline track race, combining sprint and endurance events. Omnium races for men and women are featured in the Olympics and World Championships.

Overlap Pedal overlap is the phenomenon in which the forward pedal can touch the front wheel when turned sharply. Wheel overlap is where a rider following another has his or her front wheel overlapping the lead rider's rear wheel. If the lead rider swerves, the following rider may touch wheels, often causing a crash.

Paceline A single or double line of riders, closely spaced, who take turns leading into the wind, sharing the pace, in a rotating formation. Each rider takes a pull at the front, then swings off to rest and falls back, giving each rider the chance to rest and recover while drafting .

Pantograph A style of engraving on alloy components with a bike makers' name, logos, and cut-outs, often filled in with painted colours.

Peloton The main or whole group of cyclists. Usually in racing, the main pack of riders.

Pump track A dirt or paved bike park that features twisting loops, steep mounds, and rolling sections.

Rainbow bands A symbol of the Union Cycliste Internationale (UCI), the governing body of cycling, the multicolour bands – blue, red, black, yellow, green – represent all the colours of the world's cycling nations. A rainbow jersey is the honorary jersey with rainbow bands, awarded to world champions.

Randonnée (or Rando) From the Fench for long trip. A type of organized ride, featuring distances of 200 to 1000 kilometres and designated check points. A person who rides a randonnée is a randonneur (male) or randonneuse (female).

Seat cluster Area on the bike frame at the joint of seat tube, seat stays, and top tube, including seat post clamp and seat binder bolt.

Speed wobble (or Shimmy) A phenomenon in which a bike makes an oscillating motion with the handlebars. It often occurs on a smooth straight slope and is generally considered normal behaviour for a perfectly aligned bike. It can be stopped by leaning a knee onto the top tube, or shifting one's centre of gravity.

Spinning The rapid leg speed of a cyclist's pedalling cadence, usually at or above 90 revolutions per minute (RPM). Also, a popular kind of fitness exercise on a stationary bike, often held as a class by a physical trainer.

Sweep A support rider who takes up the rear of a group ride, the last rider

Torque A measurement of force or power, as in the pedal-power torque of a cyclist, or the twisting force of a bolt or screw. A torque wrench is used to apply the proper amount of force in bike mechanics.

Trackstand A technique of balancing in place. Originally, this referred to a track-sprint race where riders jockey for position by standing on the pedals and twisting the front wheel.

Trail (1) A foot path or unpaved road, which may be dedicated for cyclists or open use for hikers and horseback riders. **(2)** The distance between the front wheel's axle and the fork's steering line and the wheel's axle.

Vert A vertical wall in a bike park with a curved base.

Wheelbase A measure of bike length based on the distance between the front wheel axle and the rear wheel axle. Most adult-size bikes have a wheelbase within the range of 36 to 45 inches long.

Index